Changing The Face of British Dance

Fifty years of London Contemporary Dance School

For Alastair, Laura, Chloë and Jack

Changing The Face Of British Dance

Fifty years of London Contemporary Dance School

Henrietta and Richard Bannerman

DANCE BOOKS

Published in 2019 by:

Dance Books Ltd
Southwold House
Isington Road
Binsted
Hampshire
GU34 4PH

© 2019 Henrietta and Richard Bannerman

ISBN: 978-1-85273-180-9

Contents

Acknowledgements		vi
Illustrations		viii
Introduction		1
Chapter 1:	The spark that lit the flame *– the 1950s and early 1960s*	5
Chapter 2:	The School finds its first home *– 1966*	11
Chapter 3:	Robert Cohan makes his mark *– 1967*	18
Chapter 4:	The move to The Place *– 1969*	23
Chapter 5:	Strong leaders and creative students *– the early 1970s*	32
Chapter 6:	Expansion secured, crisis averted *– the mid to late 1970s*	43
Chapter 7:	A new principal and a piece of paper *– the early 1980s*	52
Chapter 8:	The Graham connection loosens: changes and departures *– the mid to late 1980s*	61
Chapter 9:	A new focus for the School: the Company closes *– the 1990s*	71
Chapter 10:	Rebuilding, modernising and the creation of the CDD *– the end of the 1990s*	79
Chapter 11:	Embracing the independent dance artist – *the new millennium*	86
Chapter 12:	Fifty years on – and counting...	92
Bibliography		103
Index		108

Acknowledgements

This account of London Contemporary Dance School came about following a suggestion by the former Principal of LCDS Veronica Lewis, CBE, to mark the 50th anniversary of the School. The School, which was founded in 1966 but moved to its permanent home at The Place in 1969, was the first to be dedicated to teaching the Martha Graham style of contemporary dance in the United Kingdom. The current Chief Executive of Contemporary Dance Trust and Interim Principal of LCDS, Clare Connor, has given every encouragement to the authors to complete the story of this enterprise. The publication forms part of the celebrations for the double anniversaries of The Place and the School in 2019.

We are very grateful for the considerable support and generous contribution from many people who have been associated with the School through its successive phases, and in particular would like to thank all the people who were willing to talk to us about their own experiences and memories of their time at LCDS. Although Robin Howard, CBE, the founding father of the whole enterprise, died in 1989, both Sir Robert Cohan, CBE, and Janet 'Mop' Eager, MBE, reminded us of his vision, his commitment and the financial sacrifices he undertook to make the vision a reality. As the two remaining founding architects of the venture, they gave us an invaluable insight into the early days and the energy and determination it took to set the School on its course.

Other first-hand testimonies were given by an array of leading figures in the world of dance who have contributed educationally and artistically to the School over the fifty years, and whose careers were often formed within its studios and classrooms. These movers and shakers include the pioneering full-time students, Sir Richard Alston, CBE, and Siobhan Davies, CBE, Executive Director Sue Hoyle, OBE, the Chief Executives Kenneth Olumuyiwa Tharp, CBE, and Clare Connor, LCDS Principals Dr Richard Ralph and Professor Veronica Lewis, CBE, pianist and Head Accompanist Judyth Knight, and the senior managers, teachers, choreographers and dancers, connected to LCDS in their different ways: Kirsty Alexander, Pernille Charrington, Peter Connell, James Cousins, Anne Donnelly, Ben Duke, Mary Evelyn, Kate Flatt, Anca Frankenhaeuser, Alex Graham, Patrick Harding-Irmer, Martin Lawrance, Sue MacLennan, Namron, Rick Nodine, Chisato Ohno, Hilary Stainsby, David Steele, Isabel Tamen, and Anthony van Laast, CBE.

We are indebted particularly to former Principal Richard Ralph who scrutinised the drafts for errors we knew we would make, and to others who gave their time and knowledge generously. And we are of course grateful for the enthusiasm of David Leonard, who has devoted so much of his time and energy to publishing books about the world of dance in the UK through Dance Books.

We are grateful too to the photographers who have charted the course of the School over the years. We have tried to find the copyright holders of all the photographs, but it hasn't always been possible. So if you believe you are the copyright holder of any image please get in touch with the publisher or authors.

The School has long held a place in our own lives, not least as we – the joint authors of this book – met at its first premises in Berners Place in 1968, and married a few years later. Henrietta Lyons officially worked as School Secretary, but also taught technique and choreography, and made dances for the early workshops. Richard Bannerman was Promotion Secretary, which covered a wide range of duties, including publicity and bookings, as well as the roles of fundraiser, Company minibus driver and occasional presenter of the London Contemporary Dance Group programme. Richard left in August 1969 but Henrietta taught in the first months of The Place, before raising a family, and returning to the School in 2005. So we undertook with gratitude the invitation to trace the journey of the School from its original setting in that unimpressive but legendary cul-de-sac in Berners Place, London W1, to its impressive premises in Euston, where, under the twin arching roofs of Dukes Rd and Flaxman Terrace it has become an inseparable part of The Place.

Illustrations

Front cover: Dancers silhouetted at night time above the entrance to LCDS. Photo © Dennis Gilbert/VIEW
Back cover: Student graduation performance in 2012. Photo © Benedict Johnson.

Between pages 22 and 23

1. Robin Howard at Berners Place c.1966 with his statuette of Nijinsky by Rodin.
2. Robert Cohan and 'Mop' Eager in the 1980s.
3. lt. to rt. Dame Marie Rambert, Peter Williams, Editor of *Dance & Dancers*, Robert Cohan, and Martha Graham c.1960s.
4. Pages from the first Contemporary Ballet Trust brochure.
5. The Robin Howard Trust announces the arrival of the London School of Contemporary Dance in an advertisement placed in *Dancing Times* in February 1966.
6. The School found its first home at the far end of Berners Place, a cul-de-sac just off London's Oxford St.
7. A Graham technique class in the single studio in Berners Place in 1967.
8. Leaflets promoting the School were left for audiences during the Martha Graham Company season at the Saville Theatre in April 1967.
9. William Louther teaching at Berners Place in 1967.
10. Anna Mittelholzer teaching a class in 1967, with lt. to rt. Henrietta Lyons, Dinah Goodes, Anna Mittelholzer, and Clare Duncan.
11. On the other side of the leaflet were the aims and aspirations of the new school and its dedication to creating a 'British style of contemporary dance'.
12. Robert Cohan rehearsing Noemi Lapsezon and Robert Powell in *Sky*, which received its premiere on October 10, the first night of the season.
13. The poster advertising the inaugural performances by 'The Contemporary Dance Group and Students of The London School of Contemporary Dance' in October 1967.
14. The former drill hall and HQ of the Artists Rifles at 17 Dukes Rd, Euston, became The Place and the second home of LCDS in 1969.
15. Robin Howard announcing plans on 16 January 1969 for developing

the Artists Rifles HQ, with, among others, the first Principal of the School, Patricia Hutchinson.
16. With Robin Howard for the announcement of plans for The Place are Siobhan Davies, Mop Eager, and Robert Cohan.
17. Publicity photograph before the auction of Robin Howard's vintage cars in May 1969.
18. Choreographer Richard Alston's first work *Transit* made in 1968.
19. The programme cover of *Explorations* in July 1969, the first event at The Place.
20. One of the events at *Explorations* by artist Peter Logan, *Corridor and a Room for Robin Howard*.
21. Anthony van Laast teaching students at The Place in the 1970s.
22. Namron demonstrating class floorwork at the Residency in Hull in January 1976.
23. Jane Dudley teaching at LCDS in 1985.
24. Siobhan Davies performing 'Harmonica Breakdown' for LCDT in 1977, choreographed by Jane Dudley (1938).

Between pages 54 and 55

25. Nina Fonaroff, Head of Choreography, teaching students in 1985.
26. Viola Farber in class with LCDS students c. 1984.
27. Robert Cohan with Kenneth Olumuyiwa Tharp and Sue Booker in the 1980s.
28. Juliet Fisher teaching in 1985.
29. The Three Degrees. Receiving their degrees at the University of Kent in 1985, Charlotte Kirkpatrick, Patrick Harding-Irmer, Anca Frankenhaeuser.
30. Robert Cohan's *Stabat Mater* performed by LCDS students at Southwark Cathedral in 1983.
31. Richard Ralph, Principal of LCDS from 1979 to 1996.
32. Judyth Knight, Chief Accompanist at the School, from 1966 to 1997.
33. Susan McGuire, Head of Contemporary Dance Studies 1991 to 1998.
34. Jane Dudley and Susan McGuire with airborne students Paul Liburd and Henri Oguike in the 1990s.
35. Kenneth Olumuyiwa Tharp in Dharshan Singh Bhuller's *The Smouldering Suit* in 1988.
36. The first entrance to the School on Flaxman Terrace.
37. The new glass-fronted entrance to the School opened in 2001.
38. The Robert Cohan Studio built above the original LCDS premises.
39. Incoming Principal of the School Veronica Lewis with Assistant Principal Peter Connell in September 1998.

40. Students in the 'stretching zone' above the new entrance.
41. Doris Humphrey's *The Shakers* from 1931, restaged at LCDS in 1985.
42. Crystal Pite's *Polaris* in 2014 at Sadlers Wells with students from LCDS and Central School of Ballet.
43. Pytt Geddes taught Tai Chi at LCDS from 1970 to 1996.
44. Chisato Ohno began teaching Gaga in London in 2005 and joined the LCDS faculty in 2013.
45. Richard Alston in 2014. One of the first full-time students in 1967, Alston continued a close association with The Place and the School, and was knighted in 2019.
46. Veronica Lewis, Principal of the School from 1998 to 2018.
47. Martin Lawrance, who graduated from the School in 1993, rehearses Liam Riddick in 2010.
48. Rick Nodine, teacher of Contact Improvisation at LCDS from 2001, performing his Place Prize work *Dead Gig* in 2012.
49. James Cousins formed his own company in 2014, four years after graduating from the School.
50. Clare Connor, was appointed Chief Executive of CDT and Interim Principal of the School in 2017.

Introduction

Take a short walk along Flaxman Terrace just off the Euston Road in London, and you arrive at an impressive glass-fronted entrance and a sign which reads The Place, and immediately below it London Contemporary Dance School. It's over fifty years since the School opened its first tiny premises in 1966, 'the only School in Europe officially authorized by Miss Graham to teach her technique and approach to dance.'[1] It was down an unprepossessing mews off London's Oxford Street, where a rickety staircase led to one studio, grubby changing rooms, and a couple of offices. The Flaxman Terrace building, its current home, opens into a modern foyer, with welcoming people on reception, a tv monitor showing dancers in action, and lifts and stairs to the upper floors. The small forecourt outside is a place where students can park their bicycles or go and chat and relax between classes.

Once through the doors, there is a buzz of purposeful activity throughout the building. Dancers dash up and down the staircase that links the lower and upper regions of the School; the air is filled with the sounds of rhythmic piano and percussion jumbled together from different dance classes or rehearsals. On a stretching zone midway between the second and third floors, a young man sits in an impossibly wide box split, coaxing his extended limbs one nanometer further apart, while a young woman rolls gently around easing her back against the wooden floor. One of the second year students feels a thrill every time she walks through the School's doors: 'arriving every day I think "do I *really* go there?" But I want to live up to the standards that are here, so after putting my stuff away, I go to the studio and start warming up.'[2]

Stop at one of the studios off the staircase, and you can see dancers working at a complex phrase of Cunningham-style movement. They turn, dip and lunge before pausing precariously on one leg while the other one extends high and to the side of the body. Pass another studio on the floor above, and there's a group of students energetically falling, recovering and speedily moving across the floor in a Flying Low class. From an adjoining studio come the strange sounds of students intoning 'neeow' or 'psst' as they accompany their own unorthodox movements in an improvisation session.[3]

On the fifth floor the doors open on to a different, quieter world – the library. People sit at tables with books or journals in front of them, or are plugged into computers researching information for their essays which they are racing to complete. When it is time for a break from essays or class, a flood of students flows down to the basement to find the café, passing the wardrobe department filled with people cutting, sewing, ironing or measuring, or the body control studio where students ease a strained muscle or aching joint. The café is full to bursting with laughing, noisy young people – sitting at tables, or standing and chatting to teachers, taking the opportunity to get some tips about this or that movement. Come the evening, the café is full of dancers and theatregoers grabbing a bite before that night's performance in the Robin Howard Dance Theatre. They may have come to see student graduation presentations or experimental work by emerging choreographers in the *Resolution*, *Spring Loaded*, and *Touch Wood* seasons, or visiting companies from the UK and abroad.

As a first year student put it, LCDS is about far more than class: 'LCDS, The Place where it's situated, and the building, is not just a dance school. There's so much other stuff going on. Companies perform here, there are evening classes, there are so many people passing through, it just doesn't feel that you're cooped up in your school, you definitely feel that when you're here you're part of a much bigger network.' Another in her third year agreed: 'in London there are so many people and yet everyone is pursuing their own lives and goals – you come here and it's home. You're sharing something special. It's like being part of a community.'[4]

From the very first, LCDS was set up to be that kind of community: teachers, professional dancers and students all mingling informally. That communal atmosphere has remained constant since the earliest days. Only the scale has changed. From its basic one studio premises in the workaday cul-de-sac of Berners Place, the School has travelled a mile and a half northwards, grown to 11 studios, and in 1982 had a modest name change from The London School of Contemporary Dance to the snappier London Contemporary Dance School.[5] From an original band of 12 full-time students in 1967, the School's numbers have grown up to 180, with young people of all nationalities and backgrounds.

Over the fifty years that LCDS has existed the dance environment has evolved continuously, and the School has had to adapt. It is an opportune moment to look back and to judge what effect LCDS has had on dance in this country and further afield, and what role it plays in current contemporary dance education and practice. It has earned its reputation over successive years as a leading dance conservatoire, and its uniqueness lies in its integration with all the activities of The Place. Both LCDS and The Place are governed by Contemporary Dance Trust (CDT), created by Robin Howard in 1966. For a few years CDT was in fact CBT, Contemporary Ballet Trust, a tactical decision as Howard had been told that 'ballet would be considered artistic and educational, therefore charitable, but the word 'dance' might be assumed to mean something non-cultural and non-charitable. Only once we had been in existence for three years, and had shown what we were doing was genuinely charitable, did we dare change the name.'[6] Contemporary Dance Trust co-ordinates and is responsible for the administration of The Place, the School, the Robin Howard Dance Theatre, and all the activities and classes that take place under the two connected roofs. The Place with its theatre, studios and offices opens on to Dukes Rd while the LCDS has its separate entrance round the corner on Flaxman Terrace.

The School remains 'at the heart' of CDT,[7] managed by its own directorate and staffed by a faculty of specialists. It is integral to the operation of CDT, though since the beginning of the 21st century much of its funding support came from the Higher Education Funding Council,[8] as well as tuition fees and income from scholarships and donations. From a pioneering ambition to change the face of British dance, it has over the years established its prominence as a training-ground for dancers who can launch themselves into dance companies all over the world or into freelance careers. And from the beginning it was never only for prospective dancers. LCDS has produced a stream of choreographers from Richard Alston, Siobhan Davies and Anthony van Laast in the early years, followed by Kim Brandstrup and Aletta Collins, and on to more recent talents such as Rosie Kay, Frauke Requardt and Ben Duke.

No account of the School would be complete, however, without a reconsideration of its formation under the leadership of the businessman and dance enthusiast, Robin Howard, and the renowned ex-Graham dancer and choreographer, Robert Cohan. The span of this book therefore goes even further back to a time when the idea of a school of contemporary dance in Britain was not even a glimmer. It was in 1954 that Robin Howard discovered the Martha Graham Dance Company and it was this event that set his mind racing. It was also the year of his first sight of and meeting with Robert Cohan, then a leading dancer in Graham's company. In the spring of 1967, 13 years later, Cohan was to take his commanding part in Robin Howard's venture.

The School established its first modest premises in May 1966 and announced its opening series of classes in September that year. Even so, as Mary Clarke and Clement Crisp point out, the School at that time 'felt very much like a studio rather than a school'.[9] Although it was an unpretentious beginning, Robin Howard had assembled a distinguished array of 'Patrons of the School', which included 'Dame Ninette de Valois, DBE, Miss Martha Graham, Sir John Gielgud, The Rt Honourable the Earl of Harewood, Henry Moore, OM, CH and Dame Marie Rambert, DBE.'[10] – an impressive line-up. These early years, fuelled by Howard's passion and determination, are the point of departure for this account. The first section is devoted to the formative period of the School at Berners Place before it moved to its current Euston site in 1969. The later part addresses the recent history of LCDS, and the middle sections chart the major events in the development of LCDS during the 1970s-2000s. It traces the provision of Graham-based technique in the 1960s-1970s and the transition that took place in the late 1980s and early 1990s towards current approaches to technical and choreographic training under the label of 'somatic' practices, including Contact Improvisation.

The flourishing place of LCDS in the world of dance education and the way it has acted as a stimulus to many of the most creative forces in dance is a cause for celebration by all those interested in the development of dance into new areas. Its journey has been one of overcoming obstacles, often nudging close to the edge of a financial abyss, but, despite these challenges, continuing to evolve artistically, educationally and architecturally towards its current existence and identity.

1   Quotation from the publicity leaflet distributed at the Martha Graham Dance Company season at the Saville Theatre in 1967. Contemporary Dance Trust Archive, V&A Museum

2   Interview with second year student at LCDS, 7 December 2015

3   Dodge 2015, p.31

4   Interview with students at LCDS 2014 virtual open day Youtube

5   Mansfield 1985, p.111

6   Howard quoted in Clarke and Crisp 1989, p.18

7   Clarke and Crisp 1989, p. 9

8   HEFCE became the Office For Students in May 2018

9   Clarke and Crisp 1989, p.25

10 Contemporary Ballet Trust Letterhead 1969 – author's collection

Chapter 1

The spark that lit the flame – the 1950s and early 1960s

Robin Howard's name lives on in the Robin Howard Dance Theatre at The Place, renamed in his honour after his early death aged 65 in 1989. In the dance world he is known as the single-minded propagator of contemporary dance in the United Kingdom. Without his passion and his generosity, the widening of dance education and performance would have happened randomly and much more gradually. It was he who set the contemporary dance revolution alight, giving it a base in the founding of the School from which it expanded at an astonishing pace.

Howard came from an aristocratic family, the eldest son of Sir Arthur and Lady Howard (herself the daughter of Prime Minister Stanley Baldwin). Educated at Eton and Cambridge, the arts were always a part of his life. He collected books and manuscripts, he supported artists, he adored opera, and he loved the dance, participating in Scottish dancing in his earlier years then avidly visiting the ballet. In 1945 while serving with the Scots Guards in World War II he suffered serious injury and lost both his legs. When it was suggested to him that a slightly shorter pair of prosthetic limbs might make him more mobile, he insisted that he be restored to his full height of 6'4".[1] That bulldog determination would be called upon time and again as he fulfilled his visionary ambition to bring new dance forms to Britain: 'what I have discovered about losing my legs is an alarming tendency I already have to go it alone. I have friends and enemies like everyone. My friends call me tenacious, determined, strong-willed, my enemies call me bloody-minded, so you take it as you go!'[2]

After the war Howard studied Law at Trinity College Cambridge, but he never practised. He became involved with the United Nations Association and the Ockenden Venture, dedicated to helping war refugees, and he had a deeply spiritual, though non-religious side which underpinned what he saw as his mission in life. His knowledge and love of fine wine and food took him into the hotel business, and he bought the Gore Hotel in South Kensington in 1950, and in 1958 the country house hotel, Gravetye Manor, near East Grinstead. At the Gore he opened one of the earliest themed restaurants, called The Elizabethan Rooms. Out-of-work actors and students played the roles of serving boys and wenches, while musicians entertained guests on lutes and spinets. He displayed a more academic attitude to history with 'Shakespeare's England', his contribution to the many events marking Shakespeare's Quatercentenary in 1964, putting on show at the Gore his Folio editions of the plays as well as costumes and other documents.[3] It was at that time that a young woman found out through a friend that he was looking for an assistant. Her name was Janet Eager, 'Mop' to her friends and family. She would be his right-hand woman for the next 29 years, taking on ever more crucial roles as his involvement with dance grew and flourished.

The spark that set this passion alight was the first London season of Martha Graham's Company at the Saville theatre in the early weeks of March 1954. Alerted to the Martha Graham visit by his friend, the dancer and choreographer Peggy Harper, Howard was evidently in two minds as to whether to go. Peggy Harper arranged a meeting between Howard and her friend Robert Cohan, a leading dancer in the season, at the Gore Hotel. Cohan arrived to find Howard 'playing devil's advocate [and saying] "why should I be interested in your work. I've seen modern dance".' The two argued and Cohan 'found him difficult and irritating, and finally I said, "look I don't care whether you come or not, it's Peggy's idea and I've got to go now to a rehearsal so if you come and you enjoy it, that would be something special, but it doesn't matter to me whether you come or not." But he showed up a night or two later and he came backstage and he said, "you were right, it's the most wonderful thing".'[4]

Following this first encounter, Howard would later acknowledge that 'though I did not realise it at the time, my life was undoubtedly changed on that night. Not only did I change my immediate arrangements for the following night so I saw every performance except one, but I got to know Martha Graham and various members of the Company. Ultimately much the most important to me was Robert Cohan.'[5] Cohan felt afterwards that despite his initial resistance 'he was ready for that at that time. He was looking for something other than ballet'.[6] Howard examined his reaction and offered his own explanation: 'after the first piece I knew that this was something very important, but I wasn't at all sure it was something I liked. It wasn't until the second night, that I overcame the shock and began to come to terms with her work. Here to me for the first time in my experience was dance which genuinely spoke to every part of you on many levels. By that I mean particularly spoke to the mind as well as to the heart, or the body, or the spirit. Of the average ballet piece you can say "well, that's very beautiful but there's usually not too much to think about." I mean I can still go to classical ballet and weep at times, but the number of times that any classical ballet performance has ever made my *mind* operate I can count on the fingers of one hand.'

'It was the first time that I knew that, shall I say, my body was being excited and I was having that direct kinaesthetic feeling of contact with the dancers, that my spirit was uplifted though sometimes rather disturbed as well, and that my mind was very much engaged at the same time in working it out, but working it out in a way which didn't spoil my appreciation. The other thing which impressed me that first time, was that in every piece the whole was greater than any individual part and every piece *was* a whole. After that I was simply caught and bowled over as I have been by no other theatrical experience.'[7]

During the two-week season he would have experienced a broad range of Graham's dances, including *Appalachian Spring* (1944), Graham's evocation of the pioneers as they encountered life, faith and love, the lyrical *Diversion of Angels* (1948), and Greek-inspired dance dramas such as *Errand into the Maze* (1947),[8] a retelling of the myth of Theseus with Ariadne as the central figure. By the 1950s, Graham was renowned for the way in which she explored and staged the inner lives and thoughts of female protagonists and for the choreography she invented to express their emotions and experiences. The solo that opens *Errand* is mesmerising; Ariadne stands centre stage, arms interlocked across her abdomen and pelvis, her torso convulsing in electrified spasms that send tremors through her body. She is the very incarnation of the terror and dread that possess her as she senses the presence of the minotaur. Howard was captivated by Graham's dance theatre but it also confirmed his admiration for Robert Cohan 'as a person and as an artist at that time'.[9]

When in 1962 Howard discovered that the Graham Company was performing in Europe but that nobody would take the risk of presenting the company in Britain, he put up some of the financial backing himself, securing an invitation for Graham to appear at the Edinburgh Festival followed by a season in London at the Prince of Wales Theatre.[10] In contrast to the lukewarm reception that the company received in 1954, the performances in 1963 were a triumph, and Howard was convinced that this new 'contemporary' approach to dance was what theatre dance in the United Kingdom sorely needed. It was after the London season that Dame Marie Rambert approached Howard and said 'Mr Howard, I don't know who you are or why you've done this, but don't stop now!' Howard, through his admiration for her 'tried to do what she said, and it is only because Mim Rambert was so insistent that I did it'.[11]

Howard could have chosen other acknowledged American techniques as his core teaching requirement. Apart from Graham, the American modern dance lexicon included the widely taught technique developed by Doris Humphrey and José Limón. Other systems such as Lester Horton's was prevalent on the West Coast, while by the mid 1960s Merce Cunningham's approach was speedily gaining ground. Howard's choice of Graham stemmed no doubt from his being 'bowled over' by her choreography, and because he recognised that it established core strength and control through rigorous floor work. Principles such as the contraction and release and the 'breathings' developed spinal articulation and stability and gave the body the means of emotional and dramatic expression.

Although British dance had long benefitted from modern approaches to dance, by the 1960s there was no strong presence of modern dance performance available to British audiences. Graham's repertory offered a theatrical and compelling experience, and the American companies which followed in Graham's footsteps in 1964, led by Paul Taylor, Merce Cunningham and Alvin Ailey, continued to introduce British audiences to the variety, excitement and challenges of American contemporary dance. Homegrown companies like Peter Darrell's Western Theatre Ballet were taking ballet into new territory, and Ballet Rambert underwent a radical change of direction in 1966 when Norman Morrice became Associate Director and brought his knowledge of Graham and other American techniques to the repertory.[12]

But Howard, already in 1963, having established a close friendship with Graham, had thought of ways of bringing Graham-based training to British dancers. The idea of founding a British school had begun to form in his mind. Howard asked Graham to grant scholarships that, together with travel expenses and maintenance provided by Howard, were awarded to three students in 1963, with others following in 1964-1965.[13] Out of this initiative grew The Robin Howard Trust with the aim of showing 'what the Martha Graham approach and technique really was, to test if it was suitable for Britain, and if so to determine how'.[14] The press release concluded that 'a small committee headed by Dame Marie Rambert advised the Howard Trust on the experiment and finally recommended the establishment of a School of Contemporary Dance'.[15] As well as subsidising British dancers to study in New York, Howard brought Americans to London to give classes in Graham technique, and in 1966 announced a demonstration of 'simple classwork and combinations' to be held at Queen Alexandra's House in Kensington Gore on 20 April and 7 May. Howard was keen to point out that this was not a public performance 'as we are not ready for this yet', but it would include 'more advanced work with Patricia Christopher and our resident teachers'.[16] At this event Howard also hoped to announce 'the formation of a new and larger trust and a permanent School of Contemporary Dance'.[17] The Robin Howard Trust had completed its 'experiment'.

Eager remembers how chaotic these early days were: 'we brought dancers from the Graham Company – Mary Hinkson, Bertram Ross and

Ethel Winter. We rented space all round town. At the end of the day, I had my minivan and I put the lino down in a different place every night of the week – Mercury Theatre Notting Hill on a Monday, the Arts Educational Trust at Hyde Park Corner on a Tuesday and Wednesday afternoon, the Africa Centre in Covent Garden on Thursday, and we went back to the Mercury Theatre on Friday, and on Saturday morning I rented Victor Silvester's ballroom in Kings Road, Chelsea. We had no idea what the demand for these classes would be and when it turned out to be 200 people, we decided to audition and not take just take anybody. There were Beginners, Elementary and Intermediate, and I seem to remember we said they had to do three classes a week if they wanted to come. The classes were about a pound a time, and it went extraordinarily well.'[18]

In these few years Howard's ambition had gained unstoppable momentum, even though he was warned by Martha Graham that 'everyone is going to hate you and you'll be broke'.[19] Her words were prophetic. Over the course of the next thirty years Howard's collection of art, literature, vintage cars and property was slowly absorbed by the demands of his calling. But by May 1966 there was one pressing requirement – a permanent studio.

1   Clarke and Crisp 1989, p.13 and personal information

2   City Lights in Contemporary Dance Trust Archive, V&A Museum

3   Interview with Eager, July 2015

4   Interview with Cohan, August 2015

5   Interview with Howard, 1974, for Oral history Project, Dance Collection, New York Public Library

6   Interview with Cohan, August 2015

7   Interview with Howard, 1974, for Oral history Project, Dance Collection, New York Public Library

8   Coton, 1954, p.407

9   Howard in Jackson 2013, p.73

10   Clarke and Crisp 1989, pp.16-17

11   Clarke and Crisp 1989, p.16. Dame Marie Rambert continued to support Howard's plans, serving on the committee of the Robin Howard Trust in 1964 and 1965 before becoming a Patron of the School.

12   Norman Morrice invited the American choreographer and former dancer with the Graham Company, Glen Tetley, to mount his works on the re-modelled company. In 1967 *Ricercare* (1966) and *Pierrot Lunaire* (1962) were the first works to be performed.

13   Adshead and Mansfield 1985, p.1

14   Press release dated 1965 at Contemporary Dance Trust Archive, V&A Museum

15   Ibid.

16   Report detailing the work of The Robin Howard Trust (March 1966). Patricia Christopher was teaching at the Martha Graham School, and the 'resident teachers' were Eileen Cropley, Anna Mittelholzer, Clover Roope, and Timothy Hext. Contemporary Dance Trust Archive, V&A Museum.

17   Ibid.

18   Interview with Janet Eager, July 2015

19   Robert Cohan quoting Martha Graham Contemporary Dance Trust Archive, V&A Museum

Chapter 2

The School finds its first home – 1966

The search for the School's first premises found Howard and Eager scouring every corner of London: 'Robin and I used to drive around at weekends in the minivan looking endlessly for properties all over London. We looked at various halls, we looked at empty churches, we looked at a church in Covent Garden; there was a Methodist chapel, we looked at that. We just drove around much further out from the centre, but eventually an estate agent sent us details of a property in Berners Place, a back alley off Oxford St.'[1]

In the spring of 1966, a lease was signed and 5-7 Berners Place duly became the School's first home, an arrival noted by that month's edition of *Dance and Dancers*: 'Robin Howard's new venture will be called The London School of Contemporary Dance .... It may take time for the results of all this to become apparent, but it has all the signs of those unassuming academies formed by Dames Ninette de Valois and Marie Rambert way back in the twenties – and we all know where they led to.'[2]

Berners Place was in an area which was at that time colonised by the rag trade. These were small independent companies supplying fashions, fittings and accessories for the cheaper end of the business. Suddenly on their doorstep they began to see aspiring dancers disappearing upstairs into the first floor where they pulled on tights and legwarmers before entering the one spacious studio knocked out of a number of small workrooms. The early days in Berners Place were etched into Eager's memory: 'we shared it with a furrier. The furrier had the floor above us and we shared a bathroom-cum-lavatory with them. And we also shared the caretaker, Mr Neil, who fried his breakfast in the same fat for weeks and weeks, and it stank. Every so often I had to report to Robin that the cash box with a small padlock on it had been stolen from my little cupboard in the office. Robin said "don't call the police, Mr Neil has it".'[3]

Richard Alston, who joined LCDS in 1967 aged 19, was one of the first full-time students and discovered a jumble of people and businesses that was far from the rigour and skill that the recently arrived school was intending to foster: 'at the end of this cul-de-sac littered with rubbish bins, there was this door with a hanging sign outside saying London School of Contemporary Dance. It really was a kind of working environment, where there were all these Cypriot dressmakers. You walked up the stairs, passed one of the workrooms, went in through another door and there was one of these places which had all those old-fashioned partitions with frosted glass windows. Robin's office was to the right, the changing room was straight ahead.'[4] Berners Place looks very different today with the rabbit warren of offices and work spaces mostly redeveloped as smart mews flats and houses.

In the earliest days the School was more a base for classes, and attracted a mixture of people from different age groups and walks of life – art students, ice skaters, ballet dancers, gymnasts – many of whom had tracked down the classes that, before Berners Place, had been spread across London. One of these was Namron, who would go on to be a founder member of London Contemporary Dance Theatre, and performed with the Company for 18 years. While a scholarship student at the Rambert School, he had seen the Martha Graham Company perform in London, and had noticed signs advertising classes in Martha Graham technique: 'I thought.... wow....I'm going to try this, I got to go. It said "audition", and I managed to get one. I got to the class and I was on the floor, and I thought, oh... floor work. I tried to sit on the floor, and, you know the position, soles of the feet together, go over, bounce.....impossible! Eventually we stood up and I was more comfortable. Class finished, and I said "will I hear from you?". ..... I'm still waiting. I failed.' Caught by the buzz of excitement, he was undaunted: 'I heard they'd found premises over in Berners Place. I went across and did the classes, and I started to really get into it, and my body started to change. I was at Rambert, in my second year, but I was drifting over to Berners Place, and eventually I made the break.'[5]

There were few amenities for these keen students and certainly no showers. As for changing rooms, Eager recalls 'there was just a curtain between boys and girls, and the poor visiting teachers had to undress in another tiny and very cluttered space.'[6] But up a small flight of stairs a dance studio space measuring some 60 by 30 ft had been created. This became the jewel in the rudimentary crown of Berners Place, and Howard commissioned a floor made from one of the best surfaces for dancers – Canadian maple wood. The noise of dancers and music that came out of this busy studio produced constant complaints, and, when it rained, buckets had to be placed on the piano to catch water from the leaking roof.[7] Nevertheless these premises were alive with dancing and creative endeavour. Martha Graham had agreed to be the artistic advisor and generously provided members of her company as teachers, such as Yuriko Kikuchi (Yuriko), Robert Powell, Ethel Winter and Bill Louther.[8] Graham's patronage was a coup since it gave LCDS the flagship status of being able to claim a direct connection to the Graham School and the most experienced teachers of her technique at that particular time.

Now that there was a home, Howard determined that minds would be stretched as well as bodies. One smallish room was commandeered for a library, which was stocked with Howard's collection of dance books, but the main attraction was the studio with its bright, clean maple wood floor and large windows. The impression this space made on Alston is still vivid: 'it wasn't a big studio but it was light with a sprung wooden floor. It had windows on three sides and a door in the middle so that when you walked through it you were in the middle of the mirror wall – the mirrors weren't there when I first started and it was a huge shock when they arrived. I did that exercise where you are on your knees and you take a long lunge and you turn to the side and then you straighten up with your foot in tendu and there you are facing the front standing up. The first time I did that with mirrors I was traumatised.'[9] The studio was equipped with barres placed on the back wall and along the sides, accommodating the rarely taught Graham barre work and various ballet classes. On wintry days dancers put on the familiar woolly tights of the time, and needed to warm up their chilly muscles before class began. It was fashionable to wear all-over tights with trendy bell-bottoms often with colourful ankle warmers.

Berners Place coped with the many students from all sorts of backgrounds who flocked there, and the opportunity to develop performance skills as well as choreographic creativity was encouraged right from the start. This is evident from a programme of a dance performance on 27 October 1966 advertised on the leaflet as 'A Demonstration of Contemporary Dance', which took place at the International Student House near Great Portland Street in London. The programme on the night more ambitiously called the event 'Concert By London School of Contemporary Dance' and involved sixteen students, including Clare Duncan, Xenia Hribar and Norman Murray (Namron), all of whom were to become founder members of London Contemporary Dance Theatre. Excerpts from a typical Graham class, presenting exercises such as 'Triplets', 'Prances and Falls', and 'Jumps' were interspersed between existing works such as Paul Taylor's 'Hand Dance' from *Piece Period* (1962), as well as new works by Ruth Posner and Jacqui Lyons, whose *Solo* was performed by Anna Mittelholzer.[10] Mittelholzer was credited with arranging the classwork, and the 'musical improvisations' which accompanied it were by Judyth Knight, the British pianist and composer. Her wide experience of accompanying contemporary dance classes both in London and in New York at the Graham School would lead to a permanent role at the School.[11] Here, then, was a clear statement of seriousness on the part of young British artists about the commitment, discipline and creative energy that would come to characterise the School and all its achievements.

In the latter half of 1966 Berners Place was pulsating with energy and potential. It was not a bona fide School although this was to change when in September 1967 Patricia (Pat) Hutchinson (later known as Hutchinson-Mackenzie) was appointed as the first Principal. Howard already knew Hutchinson as Eager recalled: 'in 1964, Howard formed a committee to assist in planning his future projects, and Hutchinson was amongst others such as Brigitte Kelly from Rambert'. Hutchinson was Vice-Principal of the London College of Dance and Drama and had also taught at the Arts Educational School at Hyde Park Corner, one of the venues at which the pre-LCDS Graham-based classes in 1964 were held, and so she was already familiar with Howard's artistic policy and intention. Although assuming the role of Principal was 'quite a jump for her',[12] she took on the role with enthusiasm and a determination to make it work.

Alston, as one of her young devotees, considered her arrival a vital addition to the fledgling school: 'Pat was really remarkable and Robin was very clever to appoint her. It was his idea. She came from the Imperial Society of Teachers of Dancing, so she came absolutely from the establishment of ballet teachers. He knew that he had to gain respectability. He realised that she was unusually broadminded, very interested in new developments and was fascinated by the idea of contemporary dance. That's why she embraced the idea of being the Principal of the new School. She was very tall and extraordinarily elegant, with wonderful dignity, and taught ballet at Berners Place. She always used to wear this pleated kilt which was often worn by ballet teachers in those days. Hers was pleated tartan and when she wanted to demonstrate something she would sort of pick it up where the pin was and she would say 'look, you have to turn out from here, and whack her skirt back and out would come this long leg and it was pretty remarkable. She was a wonderful teacher and a liberal thinker about education which was a wonderful way to start the School.'[13]

With all her pedagogical and liberal qualities, Hutchinson was also charmingly scatty, a quality Anthony van Laast benefitted from as he arrived to do his school audition: '[Pat] suggested I do a class. I had done ballet but had little in the way of previous training. I was 16 and was late to start, but told my mother I still wanted to carry on dancing, and she knew of the LSCD and also Pat.[14] I remember doing the whole class at Berners Place, and nobody came in to watch me. At the end of the audition, I went to see Pat and I said "do you want me to be in the School?" and she said "oh Lord, we forgot to come and watch but you seem quite nice and athletic." At the time they were desperate for boys, so Pat just said, "of course you can be in the School".'[15] This was a wise move as van Laast joined London Contemporary Dance Theatre in 1971 and would become a leading international choreographer for theatre and film musicals.

Hutchinson may well have overlooked some events such as van Laast's audition because of the demands of organising a complex schedule of classes that ran from 9am to 6 pm with additional evening sessions.[16] She implemented the School's first full-time three-year course and Alston remembers the variety of what was on offer: 'we did a class at 9am and then we did lectures and then we did an evening class, because in the daytime there was only the one studio and this little red room in which we had things like flamenco, and demonstrations. Fernau Hall [the dance critic and historian] taught the history of dance and lectured on Kathak or Bhaharatnayam. Michael Finnissy [the composer] came, and we had a very interesting teacher called Alan Beattie.[17] He was also teaching at Saint Martin's [Art School] and through Alan, Robin somehow fixed it so that we did afternoon sessions at Saint Martin's. So we used to go to Saint Martin's and visit galleries. We also had lessons in historical dance.'[18] Over a year later van Laast was also inspired by the course that Hutchinson had put in place: 'I found the whole thing unbelievably exciting because we were linked to Saint Martin's, and so two or three times a week we'd go there to do an art course specially designed for us, which would include lighting, and, obviously, drawing. It was a very stimulating part of the foundation course.'[19]

The students who were the first to enrol often found out about the School through the dance grapevine. One of these was the 17-year-old Siobhan (Sue) Davies, who would become a leading figure in British contemporary dance, with her own companies and her organisation Siobhan Davies Dance. At Hammersmith College of Art in her first year as an art student she met Primavera Boman, who was doing her art MA but was connected to the dance world through her mother, the choreographer and teacher Hilde Holger. She suggested that Davies should come to a class at Berners Place, and as Davies said, 'I simply never stopped from that one class.' Davies captures the powerful hold that contemporary dance immediately had on her: 'I think I felt an understanding of being me, being human, while moving, which I had not felt before, and even that sounds more sophisticated than what was going on inside me. It somehow felt that doing this mattered.'

Howard's total commitment to his dance venture also made a deep impression on Davies: 'he was a huge presence literally physically. He was a mixture of benign and fatherly and twinkly, and passionate about a subject I knew nothing about. He had to do this thing which was introduce a form of dance into the country he loved, maybe in the postwar spirit of mending, in the spirit of altering the arts into something he felt was hugely necessary. He had found for him a very truthful expression and I think he wanted to introduce that to young people and make something large with it. He was energetically ambitious. You could feel the fire in a way.'[20]

The first stirrings of choreographic talent to emerge from the 1967 cohort of full-time students came in the form of Alston's rehearsals with four of his all-female peer group – including the 17-year-old Davies. Nearly 50 years later, Alston is modest about his early endeavours: 'I never ever lost a sense of deep gratitude to the four extraordinarily patient young women who were prepared to spend hours in the studio with me whilst I scratched my head and looked at the floor. It took me months to make a four-minute piece. Sue was one of them, Maria Casey, Odette Oliver whose father ran the Oval Theatre in Kennington, and Suzanne Skillen.'[21] This first work that Alston so painstakingly created was *Transit* (1968) and was performed at workshops given in the LAMDA Theatre in West Kensington.[22] It marked out Alston as a fresh new British talent.

Of those who were recruited for the initial full-time course, Alston was the only man amongst eleven female students including Davies, although there were older male dancers attending classes and performing in workshop performances. This first group of full-time students had nowhere to go in Berners Place to relax after the hard work they put in during classes, rehearsals and lectures. On Berners Street they found a friendly refuge at a coffee shop called Cabrelli's: 'Mr.Cabrelli knew us all and I think he had a rather soft spot for Sue. I seem to remember that we all loved that type of Italian frothy coffee – London was so different in 1967, so an Italian cafe off Oxford Street was something quite exotic and he did toasted cheese and ham sandwiches, things which were not really common or garden fare in those days and often when we had finished our evening classes, we'd all go to something called the Spaghetti House on the corner, it's still there – on Goodge Street, that was cheap and cheerful.'[23]

From the point of view of technical training, the new full-time programme of study was strongly based on the Martha Graham technique and students benefitted from members of Graham's company arriving in London to teach short courses. But as Eager points out, Graham technique was not wholly dominant even then and the students were exposed to several styles of contemporary dance: 'every time a company came through London, Robin would grab them to come and teach. The Alvin Ailey Company came, and Merce Cunningham came to teach class.'[24] With Pat Hutchinson teaching ballet and all the visiting teachers from many dance backgrounds, it was clear that even in the 1960s there was more on the School's bill of fare than Graham.

THE SCHOOL FINDS ITS FIRST HOME – 1966

1   Interview with Eager, July 2015

2   Anon quoted in Mansfield 1985, p.118

3   Interview with Eager, July 2015

4   Interview with Alston, August 2015

5   Interview with Namron, June 7 2018

6   Interview with Eager, July 2015

7   Clarke and Crisp 1989, p.25

8   Louther was a founder member of LCDT and was a popular teacher at LCDS from 1966-1972 and spasmodically in the 1980s.

9   Interview with Alston, August, 2015

10   Contemporary Dance Trust Archive, V&A Museum

11   Judyth Knight was the first musician employed by the emerging School, and at the invitation of the Graham dancer Mary Hinkson, and with the support of Howard, visited New York in 1965, playing for the Graham School and Company as well as the Juilliard School. She was Head Accompanist at LCDS from its inception until 1997, and composed the music for a number of choreographers, including *Family of Man* for Anna Mittelholzer, which was part of the landmark performances in 1967 at the Adeline Genee Theatre. She toured with the Company and the London Contemporary Dance Group, and wrote books and articles on music and dance. Interview with Knight, September 2015 and April 2019.

12   Interview with Eager, July 2015

13   Interview with Alston, August 2015

14   Van Laast's mother was the teacher and educationist, Peggy Hawkins

15   Interview with van Laast, May 2016

16   Clarke and Crisp 1989, p.25

17   Alan Beattie was awarded a scholarship to study at LCDS and contributed work to Explorations in 1969 as well as to workshops and performances.

18   Interview with Alston, August 2015

19   Interview with van Laast, May 2016

20   Interview with Davies, January 2018

21   Ibid.

22   Jordan 1992, p.26

23   Interview with Alston, August 2015

24   Interview with Eager, July 2015

Chapter 3
Robert Cohan makes his mark – 1967

1967 saw another milestone in the development of LCDS and this was the arrival of Robert Cohan. Since Robin Howard's first meeting with him during the Graham London season in 1954, Cohan had emerged as not just one of the leading dancers of the Graham Company, but also as a gifted teacher and a highly-regarded choreographer, for a time running his own Robert Cohan Dance Company. They met again in 1963 during the Company's visit to the Edinburgh Festival and London, and during the next three years Howard's plans for contemporary dance in Britain gained considerable momentum. The decisive moment – which would have far-reaching consequences for both Howard and Cohan – happened in early 1966. Howard, who had built a strong connection with Graham through his moral and financial support, found himself in New York, as a temporary – unpaid – administrative director to the Graham School and Company. In his mind also was the idea that Graham might consider releasing someone to get his plans for a British school and performance group on to a more solid basis. She suggested Cohan.[1]

A private dinner party in Graham's home was arranged, and Cohan was invited: 'Martha asked if I would come to her place and Robin was there, and that's when he formally asked me [to come to London]. I said that I would think about it. The next day I went to see Martha and I asked her "do you agree with this, do you want me to go?" and she said, "well, I think it would be good for you because I know you have the experience to handle something like that on your own", and I said "well what about here?" and she said, "don't worry about that, I think you should go, and we owe it to Robin", and I'll never forget those words. Robin was so helpful and he was so in love with it all. So I thought I would give it a go and I called it a trial. That was it, I came to try it.'[2]

When Cohan arrived in 1967, there were already well-trained British Graham practitioners teaching at LCDS. Amongst these was the dancer Anna Mittelholzer who had independently travelled to New York to study at the Martha Graham studio in the early 1960s. She claims that she returned from New York in 1965 at Howard's request expecting to play a major role in the structuring of British contemporary dance rather than remain under the domination of an American aesthetic.[3] During 1966 and early 1967 Mittelholzer was the main resident teacher, taking the major share of classes. However, Howard had realised that if he was to spearhead a major new dance form in Britain, he would need a leader with high-profile professionalism, in fact someone who was a star in the world of contemporary dance. Whilst there was a talented and knowledgeable band of British dancer-choreographers like Mittelholzer, they lacked the depth of experience and artistic authority of a leader such as Cohan. It was that deep understanding and the ability to articulate clearly what was required that struck Siobhan Davies: 'when he taught there was a kind of gravitas to what he taught. I was going to say there felt like an aura around him in terms of knowledge, experience, depth, but I also remember a playfulness. I think Bob also introduced the idea that working hard as a discipline was a good thing, and the harder you worked the more you learnt and the more you learnt the more you could do. To be in touch with that aged 17 and 18 was all-encompassing.'[4]

Cohan brought a calm but authoritative approach to Graham-based technique and held firm views as to how he should proceed in this new and unformed teaching environment with its pool of raw talent: 'it was very clear to me that we couldn't transplant Graham *per se* and that I would have to teach it my way because it was obviously different immediately. Firstly, the floors were cold so how could you spend 35 minutes on a cold floor? I had to raise the temperature everywhere and Robin was horrified at the bills. He said "but they can warm up, they can wear clothes". I said "no, they can't wear clothes, I want to see their bodies". The studio has to be warm enough so they don't spend half the class getting warm.'

'The teachers all took my classes, that's the way I wanted to do it, and every once in a while, I had a teachers' class so that we were all teaching the same thing – not mixing up counts too much – people were free to do what they wanted but I didn't want people saying something radically different from what I would say or what the Graham technique was about – especially in things like the contraction and the release and gravity and the turning out, and where it came from and all the basic material – that was very important in the beginning especially, because it was all new, and I was saying this is what you do. I was coming into a situation I think where people thought contemporary was free, that you could do whatever you wanted – a lot of the students that came thought that.'[5]

The contraction, central to Graham's conception of dance, involves squeezing the air out of the lungs and pressing the sitting bones into the floor as one moves the pelvis by engaging the deep abdominal muscles. The torso hollows but does not sink. This gathering of energy into the lower abdomen is followed by the often explosive *release* of energy on inhalation – an action literally capable of transporting the dancer from one side of the stage to another. It is the exhalation and intake of breath that fuels the movement – exhalation on contraction and inhalation for release. This breathing rhythm is fast or slow, percussive or sustained depending on the type of contraction/release performed, and determined by the expressive nature of the choreography. Stuart Hodes, a member of the Graham company from 1946-58, insightfully described his personal experience of Graham's basic principle of 'contraction and release': 'from deep in my pelvis I drew my body in a concave arc from hips to head, relishing the sensation of deep muscles working and the surge of force into my bones that seemed to shoot out of my flexed hands and feet. Release straightened me like an uncoiling spring.'[6]

Cohan was extremely analytical and sometimes ruthless about technical principles, threatening that he would order students to remove their tights unless he could see the inner thigh muscles working properly. These might seem draconian measures but they were essential if Cohan was to achieve the mammoth task with which Howard charged him: 'when I showed up at Berners Place in the Spring of 1967, Robin said that he wanted to have a performance in June or July and I said, "no, they won't be ready but we'll work towards September or October, we'll work all summer". And I kept saying "Robin they won't know how to dance but I'll rehearse them so much that they'll know the steps" and that was it.'[7]

The charismatic Cohan went about the preparatory work methodically and seemed utterly unfazed about shouldering the artistic and directorial burden of assembling, rehearsing and staging a full evening's programme of contemporary dance. He chose the performers from those attending classes at Berners Place, matching their varied levels of experience with what was required on stage. After a concentrated period of work, in October 1967, and bolstered by the expertise of the Graham dancers Noemi Lapsezon and Robert Powell, Howard's Contemporary Ballet Trust presented the Contemporary Dance Group in *Dance One, Two, Four* at the Adeline Genée Theatre, East Grinstead, thus launching what was destined to become London Contemporary Dance Theatre.

These performances in themselves were a significant statement of the arrival of British contemporary dance, and that initial performance on 10 October also put down a defining marker for the developing School, with the young students inspired by the powerful performances as well as by the starry stage presence of Lapsezon, Powell and Cohan himself, who danced with Powell in *Hunter of Angels*, a duet he had choreographed in 1959.[8]

Howard's intention as realised by Cohan was to 'display some of the creative work which was already an important aspect of the School's identity,'[9] and, with this in mind, emerging talent in the form of Mittelholzer's *Family of Man* and Patrick Steede's *Piece for Metronome and Three Dancers* was seen alongside the seasoned Cohan's *Hunter of Angels, Tsaikerk, Eclipse* and *Sky*. That these first performances overlapped with the beginning of the new full-time course, set the agenda for establishing an athletic, polished contemporary dance style delivered through compelling performances. For the fledgling dancers and choreographers these early performances were a seminal moment. A young Siobhan Davies, then a first year student, who had little more than a walk-on part in Mittelholzer's ensemble dance, was inspired to try out Lapsezon's movements in quiet moments of rehearsals and even in the theatre's wings.[10]

The run of five nights from 10-14 October received a warm press. *The Times* welcomed the performances of a Group who 'knows where it wants to go and has a good idea of how to get there',[11] and Alexander Bland in *The Observer* recognised that '[although] Robin Howard cautiously announced that the programme was only a preamble to the company's permanent establishment, it is clear in effect the deed is done, and that last Tuesday [10th] will be celebrated as the fateful birthday. It is fair, then, to record that the Contemporary Dance Group has got away to an excellent start.'[12] As for the local paper, the *East Grinstead Observer* wrote: 'last week the Contemporary Dance Group presented a brilliant programme, and it went like a bomb! Such was the enthusiasm that the audience literally howled for more when the final curtain descended. It was a triumph for director Robert Cohan.'[13]

While the large body of dancers waited for its first season as London Contemporary Dance Theatre in 1969, the Contemporary Dance Group, retitled the *London* Contemporary Dance Group (authors' italics), used a small number of dancers to spread the contemporary dance message across the UK, following on directly from the East Grinstead debut. From November 1967 dancers took part in a presentation, which, it was promised, 'will follow the formula developed by the Royal Ballet's *Ballet for All*'.[14] Peter Brinson's small-scale *Ballet for All* programme combined a technical demonstration with extracts from the Royal Ballet repertoire, and London Contemporary Dance Group was similarly planned to offer 'three dancers, a speaker, a stage manager and a pianist' with a demonstration of technique as well as short 'contemporary dance ballets'.[15] Over the following years the London Contemporary Dance Group offered dancers valuable performance experience as well as bringing contemporary dance to schools, colleges and theatres all over the country. In 1970 *Ballet for All* and the Group joined forces to present a combined introduction to ballet and contemporary dance, a project which ran successfully until 1972.[16]

Cohan had spearheaded both the Adeline Genée performances and the development of the Group, but at this time he was not planning a long-term stay in London. As co-director of the Graham Company he was needed back in New York. So in 1967 he felt torn between his life in America and the burgeoning British contemporary dance scene: '[after the Adeline

Genée performances] I went right back to New York and worked with Martha and I came back a couple of times to London in between. Then we had a meeting, and I remember dancers like Clare [Duncan], Xenia [Hribar] and Namron who spoke up and said "it was going to be very hard to have a company with an artistic director who isn't here", and I said that I was still working with Graham in New York so let's do it bit by bit.'[17]

But there was another major incentive that would draw Cohan towards settling in London to spearhead this new and 'intoxicating' adventure.[18]

1   Jackson 2013, p.133

2   Interview with Cohan, August 2015

3   Author's personal communication with Mittleholzer, 2000

4   Interview with Davies, January 2018

5   Interview with Cohan, August 2015

6   Hodes 2002, p.67

7   Author's personal recollections and interview with Cohan, August 2015

8   See Clarke and Crisp 1989, pp.26-28

9   Clarke and Crisp 1989, p.27; Jackson 2013, pp.146-147

10   Author's personal recollection

11   *The Times* on 16 October 1967, quoted in CBT's summary of press reviews (1967), authors' collection

12   Clarke and Crisp 1989, p.29

13   *The East Grinstead Observer*, October 1967, quoted in CBT's summary of press reviews (1967), authors' collection

14   Letter sent to schools, colleges and arts organisations by Eager on 4 July 1967, Contemporary Dance Trust Archive, V&A Museum

15   Ibid.

16   See Ralph 1977, pp.25-30

17   Interview with Cohan, August 2015

18   Mackrell www.guardian.com May 2010

1. Robin Howard at Berners Place in the late 1960s with his statuette of Nijinsky by Rodin.
Photo Anthony Crickmay. ©V&A Images/Victoria and Albert Museum, London

2. The other members of the triumvirate alongside Robin Howard: Robert Cohan, founding Artistic Director, and 'Mop' Eager, executive administrator, pictured in the 1980s. Eager collection. Photo © Donald Southern/ArenaPAL

3. Three key figures who were the first supporters of Robin Howard's vision: Dame Marie Rambert, Robert Cohan and Martha Graham, with Peter Williams, Editor of *Dance and Dancers*, c. 1960s. Photo: Eager collection

The Contemporary Ballet Trust Ltd.

In 1965 a small Committee under the Chairmanship of Dame Marie Rambert supervised some experimental classes in London to assess the demand for the Teaching of Contemporary Dance.

Three members of the world-renowned Martha Graham Company gave classes for the Rambert School of Ballet, Western Theatre Ballet and the Arts Educational Trust and to some 200 individual students selected from a much larger number of applicants, as well as demonstrations for the Royal Ballet School and nine other ballet schools and clubs in various parts of the country. As a result the Committee recommended as essential the creation of a new School of Contemporary Dance in London.

This booklet describes the plans of the Contemporary Ballet Trust whose first object is to establish permanently and to endow a London School of Contemporary Dance with the highest artistic aims.

The Trust's second object is to help young choreographers learn their art in the studio and in performance.

Its other aims can be broadly stated as being to help the development of ballet and the dance as an art in the closest possible relationships to the other arts.

The Cost

£25,000 for each of the next two years is required in order for the Trust to continue its work.

At least another £250,000 will be required to establish the School permanently in its own premises and allow the Trust to fulfil its other objects.

We know that this project is important to all those concerned with the development of the arts in this country. Both we and the students to whom this is imperative, depend on your generosity to enable us to go forward.

How You Can Help

1. **By making a single gift** either towards the general funds of the Trust or for a specific object, e.g., the decoration and equipping of a Practice Room etc. etc. The Secretary will supply details of costs.

2. **By covenanting a gift.** In which case the Trust will be able to recover the Income Tax you have already paid on your donation. Under the standard rates of tax, current in August 1966, this rebate is considerable. If covenanted for 7 years:—

   £500 annually will cost you £3,500.   The Trust will get £5,957.
   £100 annually will cost you £700.   The Trust will get £1,191.
   £25 annually will cost you £175.   The Trust will get £297.
   £10 annually will cost you £70.   The Trust will get £119.

   The appropriate forms for this method of gift accompany this brochure.

3. **By presenting a Scholarship** which can be recorded in the name of the donor. The number of Scholarships required is limited and of several types, particulars of which can be obtained from the Secretary.

All cheques, Covenants and Banker's Orders should be made payable to —

CONTEMPORARY BALLET TRUST LTD.

The Secretary, ... London W.1.

---

4. and 5. In the Spring of 1966 Robin Howard and his committee issued a brochure outlining the aims of the Contemporary Ballet Trust and requesting financial help. In the February 1966 edition of the *Dancing Times* came the announcement of the establishment of The London School of Contemporary Dance.

The Trustees of the Robin Howard Trust announce that their classes in Contemporary Dance will now be taken over by the

London School of Contemporary Dance

The School is under the patronage of:
Dame Ninette de Valois D.B.E., Sir John Gielgud C.B.E., Miss Martha Graham, The Right Hon. the Earl of Harewood, Mr. Henry Moore C.B.E., and Dame Marie Rambert D.B.E.

Miss Graham has also agreed to be the Artistic Advisor. As such she is not directly responsible for policy nor teaching but she has most graciously offered to advise, to visit the School whenever in London, to encourage members of her Company to teach there and to offer scholarships in her School in New York.

Applications now being accepted for the next series of classes starting September 19th. All teachers have been regular members of the Advanced class in the Graham School in New York.

Information and application forms from the School's Secretary:
**Miss Janet Eager,
5 to 7 Berners Place, London W.1.**
Tel: (01) 580 - 1057

6. The School found its first home (1966-1969) at the far end of Berners Place, a cul-de-sac close to London's Oxford St. The area has since been completely redeveloped. Photo © Bannerman

7. A Graham technique class in the single studio in Berners Place in 1967. Namron collection. Photo © Envisaged

MARTHA GRAHAM

BERTRAM ROSS
ETHEL WINTER
ROBERT COHAN

YURIKO
ROBERT POWELL
DUDLEY WILLIAMS

MARY HINKSON
CLIVE THOMPSON
TAKAKO ASAKAWA

AND

MERCE CUNNINGHAM
DONALD McKAYLE
PAUL TAYLOR

BETTIE DE JONG
JULIET FISHER

This is not a new cast list. It is the names of the Artistic Advisor, Miss Graham, and of present and former members of her Company who have already taught for the London School of Contemporary Dance.

The School is proud to be associated with Bernard Delfont and the Martha Graham Foundation in presenting this season by the Martha Graham Company at the Saville Theatre. The School is even prouder that it is the only School in Europe officially authorised by Miss Graham to teach her technique and approach to dance.

For further information please turn the page —

8. Leaflets promoting the School were left for audiences during the Martha Graham Company season at the Saville Theatre in April 1967.

9. One of the teachers from the Graham Company, not mentioned on the handout, was William Louther, seen here at Berners Place in 1967. He danced in early LCDT performances, and taught and choreographed in the UK and internationally. Namron collection. Photo © Envisaged

Patrons: Dame Ninette de Valois, D.B.E.
Sir John Gielgud.
Miss Martha Graham.
The Rt. Hon. The Earl of Harewood.
Henry Moore, Esq., C.B.E.
Dame Marie Rambert, D.B.E.

THE LONDON SCHOOL
OF
CONTEMPORARY DANCE

is, with Miss Graham's permission and encouragement, seeking to establish a British style of Contemporary Dance based upon Miss Graham's technique and approach. Since 1963 British dancers have been specially trained in the Graham School in New York and more recently, regular classes have been held in London.

After this season at the Saville Theatre, Robert Cohan, one of Miss Graham's Co-Directors, and Robert Powell, a soloist with the company, will return to teach at the School. In the summer they will perform with teachers and students of the School in works by Mr. Cohan and by British choreographers.

For more information about The London School, about performances of Contemporary Dance—or if you can help with work or contacts or money, please fill in this form:—

NAME ....
(Block capitals please)
ADDRESS ....
....
....

Hand it to an attendant at the Theatre, or write to:
The London School of Contemporary Dance
5/7, Berners Place, London, W.1. Tel. 01-580 1057

10. Anna Mittelholzer teaching a class in 1967, lt. to rt. Henrietta Lyons, Dinah Goodes, Anna Mittelholzer, and Clare Duncan. Photo © Envisaged

11. The reverse of the flyer emphasised the aims and aspirations of the new school and its dedication to creating a 'British style of contemporary dance'.

12. Robert Cohan rehearsing Noemi Lapsezon and Robert Powell in *Sky*, which received its premiere at the Adeline Genée theatre in October 1967. Photo Anthony Crickmay. ©V&A Images/Victoria and Albert Museum, London

13. The poster advertising the landmark performances by 'The Contemporary Dance Group and Students of The London School of Contemporary Dance'.

14. Photo © Bannerman
The former drill hall and HQ of the Artists Rifles at 17 Dukes Rd, Euston, became The Place and the second home of LCDS in 1969. Robin Howard presented his plans at a press conference on 16 January 1969, with lt. to rt. architect Norman Branson, Robert Cohan, RH, first Principal of the School Patricia Hutchinson, ballet teacher Cleo Nordi, and CDT press officer Annette Massie.
15. Photo © Donald Southern/ArenaPAL

16. Also with Robin Howard were lt. to. rt. back row: Siobhan Davies, Mop Eager, UKPI representative (the owners), and unidentified. Front row: RH, Norman Branson and Robert Cohan. Photo © Donald Southern/ArenaPAL

17. Publicity photograph before the auction of Robin Howard's vintage car collection in May 1969 to provide funds for the School. In the 1914 Stellite two-seater are School students including Kiki Obermer (2nd lt.) and Celeste Dandeker (3rd lt.) with Richard Bannerman at the wheel. Photo: Bannerman collection

18. Choreographer Richard Alston's first work *Transit* made in 1968 with fellow students Siobhan Davies (facing out), Maria Casey, Odette Oliver and Suzanne Skillen. LCDS Archive. Photo © Envisaged

19 and 20. In July 1969 The Place put on its first Event: *Explorations*. Installations, performances and art took over the whole building. The artist Peter Logan invited people to walk down a narrow passage brushing past strange objects, including a naked male leg, possibly belonging to student Richard Alston. Photo ©Mitja Hinderks

21. Anthony van Laast teaching students at The Place in the 1970s. Photo Anthony Crickmay. ©V&A Images/Victoria and Albert Museum, London

22. Namron demonstrating class floorwork at the Residency in Hull in January 1976. Namron collection. Photo © Kenneth Berry Studios

23. Jane Dudley, who led the LCDS teaching faculty from 1970 to 1991, with students in 1985. Photo © Dee Conway/Bridgeman Images.

24. Siobhan Davies performing 'Harmonica Breakdown' for LCDT in 1977, the celebrated work by Jane Dudley (1938). Photo Anthony Crickmay. ©V&A Images/Victoria and Albert Museum, London

Chapter 4
The move to The Place – 1969

By early 1968, LCDS was attracting more international students including Anca Frankenhaeuser, who was destined to join the Company in 1973. She has a vivid account of her arrival: 'one of the founder LCDT dancers, Franca Telesio, came to Finland to teach a short course and recommended that I come to London, so on New Year's Eve 1968, I landed in England by cargo ship from Finland. I found my way to The London School of Contemporary Dance, as it was called then. An extraordinary man called Robin Howard drove me and my friend Ritva Lehtinen first to see Franca, who was in hospital recovering from an operation. Then he drove us all over London to give us some idea of the city before he took us to dinner. That was my introduction to a new home, where I stayed for twenty-one years.'[1] Frankenhaeuser was a part time student in 1968, living and working as an au pair in London but taking two classes a day at the School, with Pat Hutchinson, as she says, 'mothering us firmly but with compassion'.[2] She considered herself very 'fortunate' to have experienced 'the one-and-a-half studios at Berners Place, with shandy and cheesecake at Cabrelli's across the street!'

As students like Frankenhaeuser were beginning their studies at the School, Cohan was commuting between New York and London, working spasmodically with the Graham Company and returning to London to be on hand for important events, such as directing workshop performances featuring new choreography given at the LAMDA theatre.[3] Because he came and went, his appearances at the School intrigued students like van Laast, who was one of the second cohort of full-time students alongside Celeste Dandeker,[4] Chris Banner and Paula Lansley. Cohan's arrival left a lasting impression on van Laast: 'there was this mysterious man called Robert Cohan whom nobody had seen when we first started, and then one day, I think after about a term, this man walked in with long hair and jeans. This *was* the mysterious Robert Cohan, and immediately you knew you were in the presence of someone who was very special and very clever, and one could feel just by his aura why so many people were buzzing around him, and around the Company. There was a small Company then and we were taught by Bill Louther and Clover Roope,[5] with Ruth Posner as our main teacher.'[6]

As well as inspiring new students with his air of celebrity, Cohan had firm ideas about the need for a proper base so that Howard's ambitions could be realised. Most of the time when he discussed plans with Howard,

Cohan insisted, 'we have to get another place to work and it has to be big enough to have a school and a theatre'. Eager and Howard set off, once more scouring London for premises with the potential to fulfil Cohan's requirements. The hunt intensified in 1968, as it became more and more urgent to expand: 'I went with Robin to the Old Vic which was for sale and very dilapidated. Robin said it would be great and would give us a good theatre but "where the hell would we put the studios!" There was no space for studios. Also I remember going to Covent Garden, Pineapple Studios – we looked at them. We looked at endless places, even the Lyric Hammersmith. Richard Bannerman, Robin's assistant and general factotum, was also asked to inspect premises suggested by estate agents and he visited drill halls such as one in Chelsea. But one day Richard was sent to the defunct headquarters of The Artists' Rifles and he told Robin that it was very dusty but it had a lot of space. Then Robin took the actress Irene Worth there – she was one of our patrons – and she was very enthusiastic.'[7]

The Artists' Rifles Drill Hall was located at 17 Dukes Rd, London WC1, a picturesque side street leading directly off the busy Euston Rd. Richard Alston was another early visitor: 'I remember Sue [Siobhan Davies] and I came out of class and we were hovering as we used to do. Robin was in his office and he suddenly gestured to us and said "I want you to see something, are you free, have you got a lecture", and we answered "no", so he said, "I'll meet you downstairs." He hailed a cab, it was pouring with rain, and he said, "I've been looking for something for a long time and I think I've found it and I'd love you two to see it." He took us to this fine terracotta building and it took us a long time to get in because the caretaker who lived on the top floor was deaf. But when we entered we saw the rifle range with all the bullets and things in the basement, and there was the drill hall which had been used for some sort of regimental party with wilted balloons hanging from the ceiling.'[8]

Clearly new and exciting developments were in the air and the news was communicated to Cohan that a space had been found which 'seemed to have what I wanted, a studio, and a theatre, and Robin was very excited about it, so if he went ahead and got the place, I had to be here'. By Christmas 1968 Cohan had made the momentous decision that he would come to London permanently, and he came with ambition: 'we worked all through the summer of 1969 preparing for our season [at The Place]. I was here in London to stay.'[9]

From August 1968, Howard had been busy negotiating a 21-year lease, but the owners retained the right to redevelop the property in 1977, halfway through the duration of the lease, a shadow which loomed over the future of both the Company and the School. Nevertheless, on 16

January 1969 a bold press release announced the proposed arrival of a 'new arts centre in London within the next two months'[10] and gave significant details about the aims, intentions and prospective layout of the centre. The press and guests arrived for the opening ceremony, unaware that a moment of high drama was about to happen.

It was yet another instance, as Eager remembers, when Howard's bulldog stubbornness prevailed: 'there was a press conference in the empty theatre with Robin announcing we had got this place. We were sitting at the table about to sign the lease, and David Reynolds from the Arts Council came in, handed Robin a letter and said "Mr Howard, before you sign this, I think you had better read this letter." Robin opened the letter and found that it said there would be no more money from the Arts Council. Robin closed it up, sealed the letter and signed the lease. Later he announced, "well, unfortunately the Arts Council has said there'll be no money, so unless there's £30,000 from somewhere, we may have to close the building".'[11]

Howard's gamble was vindicated when he received a telephone call from the Gulbenkian Foundation in Britain telling him that if he could keep the whole enterprise going until April, the Foundation would provide the much needed £30,000 over three years,[12] and, undaunted by the negative attitude of the Arts Council, which did eventually offer more funds, Howard pressed ahead with his plans. The conversion of the old Artists' Rifles Drill Hall began. Van Laast was part of the unofficial building team: 'in our third term at Berners Place, Robin had bought the Artists Rifles building, so a lot of us in the afternoons would go to The Place and do painting, decorating, working with Norberto [Chiesa] and part of the team who built the theatre. At the end of my third term I was spending more time working at The Place than doing classes. So I then went on my Greek holiday and when I came back we'd moved to The Place.'[13] Frankenhaeuser, also involved in the initial cleaning and painting of these new premises, found that 'after Berners Place, The Artists' Rifles seemed like a castle full of wonderful possibilities'.[14]

Alston was equally struck by the speed at which everything happened: 'the next time we went there, all these amazing floors had been laid. Bob was the guru in those days and Bob had said that the floors had to be Canadian maple and you had to lay them in a specific way – he knew exactly how it had to be done. We had studio 4, which became the company studio facing the car park. We had one with no windows called studio 5, those both had sprung wooden floors. Studio 3 had been the officers' mess and I think it already had a wooden floor in the front with the beautiful windows. They put a breeze block wall in the drill hall and that was studio 2. Studio 1 was the stage because we used to have classes in there, studio 6 was what is now the theatre office and that had a parquet floor which wasn't sprung so that was always tricky. There were lots of studios and lots of space so that was really exciting.'[15]

Eager was equally impressed by the way some of the Drill Hall's original fittings and fixtures were commandeered: 'in the basement was an old shooting range. And the wooden things where the students used to keep their clothes was exactly where the soldiers used to keep their guns. And the top floor was turned into the restaurant managed by Michael Mortimer who ran The Black Sheep cafe round the corner from Dukes Road.'[16]

These new premises, initially called Artists' Place, in a nod to the former occupation by the Artists' Rifles, soon became known as The Place. It was first shown off to the public through an event masterminded by Howard in July 1969. As well as displaying his new building, Howard enjoyed offering visitors the unexpected and experimental aspects of his approach to the arts and to British contemporary dance. Similar to a 'happening', *Explorations* occupied the entire building and embraced the participation of visual artists as well as choreographers. The sculptor, Peter Logan provided an installation called *Corridor and a Room for Robin Howard* (1969), and one of those setting off on this unpredictable journey was the dance scholar and writer Stephanie Jordan: 'spectators walked down a long corridor brushing past various moving objects, including a huge coiled spring from which emerged coloured streamers, and a naked leg [belonging to Alston] protruding through an apparently solid wall. Then they entered a room where a mechanical ballet took place.'[17]

Adding his own contribution to the event, the visual artist, Derek Jarman, provided a 'guest costume,' consisting mainly of ribbons,[18] and to begin the second programme the Argentinian artist, Leopoldo Maler created *'X'It'*, 'a large work for sixteen performers and fork-lift trucks which lifted audience members into their seats'.[19] This surreal event so redolent of the late 1960s anticipated the collaborative pathways the School would go on to explore. Whilst the choreography on show in the various *Explorations* events was reputedly 'unsophisticated',[20] Howard foresaw a broadening of artistic and choreographic approach that would pave the way for further site-specific work and conceptual dance.

The serious and more polished side of this new form of British contemporary dance was unveiled at The Place in September 1969. Officially opened on 2 September by the then Chairman of the Arts Council, Lord Goodman, it heralded the first performance of the Company in its own theatre.[21] The ensuing three-week season presented Graham's *El Penitente* (1941), and Alvin Ailey's *Hermit Songs* (1961). Cohan provided several pieces – the most significant of which was the specially choreographed *Cell*, and there were also dances by the British Clover

Roope and the Australian Barry Moreland.

These were heady times of excitement and promising new departures. Van Laast remembers his first experience of *Cell* as 'the most explosive theatrical moment' he had ever witnessed.[22] Frankenhaeuser, by then a full-time student, recalls long stints helping out in the wardrobe department, 'hemming Bob Powell's *El Penitente* trousers until my fingers were bleeding'. She also remembers the perk of working in the newly opened restaurant, as its owner, Michael Mortimer, let the student helpers, once the pre-show rush was over, 'nip down to stand at the back of the theatre and watch whatever was on, as long as we came straight back to clear up during the interval and then serve dessert after the show. This was how I saw the opening night of *Cell*. What an experience!'[23]

Even though this was an undoubtedly inspiring and exciting time for the students, Eager speaks of this first era as a 'terrible time' because of the severe financial problems that beset the organisation. Most of the funding was provided by Howard. In May 1969 he sold his collection of vintage cars, and sounded a gloomy note in his preface to the September 1969 season programme designed by Norberto Chiesa, featuring the by-line: '1969 – Year of The Place.'[24] It was a period of high achievement for Cohan and the Company, but Howard wrote: '[we] cannot continue without money from somewhere. Unless money is found by Christmas, the Trust must close down. It is hard to believe that Britain cannot find at least as much money for its only contemporary dance organisation as it finds for eight or nine ballet organisations, each of which on average receives over five times as much as we do.'[25]

Howard's downbeat forecast for the future of both School and Company had been brightened somewhat by the Gulbenkian Foundation's offer of £30,000 over three years payable from April 1970, as mentioned earlier, and followed by the Arts Council retracting its refusal to provide increased funding and stepping into the breach with a promise to increase its grant to £20,000 in April 1970.[26] So, by the autumn term of 1969, the Trust, School and Company were installed in their new premises at Euston, with its extra space housing the all-important theatre, six studios, better changing rooms, an onsite café, and what at the time in Britain was an entirely new resource, a Pilates studio. Howard was aware of the benefits of Joseph Pilates' work in both enhancing technical efficiency and for dancers working through injury. He had experienced this in New York when he saw how important such a facility had become to the dance fraternity there, including the Graham Company. Howard wanted to recruit a volunteer from the students attending classes at Berners Place to learn and practise this work, and a young teacher and aspiring dancer, Alan Herdman, responded to Howard's invitation.

Herdman travelled to New York and studied intensively with Carola Trier and Bob Fitzgerald, two instructors who had been trained by Pilates himself, and returned thoroughly steeped in the Joseph Pilates Method. There followed, in The Artists' Place Society News of December 1970, an announcement that a 'new service for members' in the form of a 'body conditioning and corrective exercise studio' would be available, run by 'Robert Fitzgerald from New York, assisted by Alan Herdman'. Hour-long 'supervised' sessions of 'exercises on specially designed apparatus which develop maximum strength and flexibility' were described as being 'particularly useful for people trying to get in shape for skiing or horseback riding, or who simply feel unfit'. The fee was £2 per session for all Society members (except Theatre members), £3 for others. Once up and running, LCDT dancers, faculty and students were invited to sample this new exercise phenomenon to great advantage. It is fair to claim that Fitzgerald and Herdman introduced the first generation of British dancers, singers, actors and people from all walks of life to 'Pilates'. Given the diversity and widespread popularity of this practice in 21st century Britain, it hardly seems credible that British Pilates was launched in 1970 at The Place.[27]

Although there was an exponential increase in the number of studios in the Duke's Road premises, these new spaces had to be shared, and some of them were rented out to others. Performances at the theatre had to be limited to an audience of members only, so anyone wanting to attend performances in the 1970s joined The Artists' Place Society and was issued with a membership card. Although the theatre would be used by the Company, Group and Workshops, it would also be available for rent. Studio 2 as described earlier by Alston was to become a permanent classical ballet studio for classes given by the ex-Pavlova Company dancer, Cléo Nordi. The Place was also to be the headquarters of the Pierrot Players, founded by the composers Peter Maxwell Davies and Harrison Birtwistle.[28]

Howard envisaged a project which would foster an atmosphere of 'co-operation between the arts'.[29] Alston recalls the time just after his graduation in 1970 when he was given the job of running the theatre box office, and through that discovered the diversity of contemporary music and theatre performed there. However, one of the regular events appealed to a different clientele: 'it was something called the New Cinema Club, and it came on Mondays. As a box office attendant, it was my job to go down the stairs into the bowels of the basement and knock on the door of the ladies' changing room and say "ladies, remember it's Monday night and it's dirty mac night and just be careful", because the male cinemagoers used to always wander down the corridor, glasses all steamed up, saying, "I seem to have got completely lost, I'm looking for the cinema." It became a regular thing.'[30]

The Place at this time was also the home of the art-school trained Geoff Moore's *Moving Being* where he experimented with early forms of multimedia performance or collage, juxtaposing dance, photographic slides, text, music and sound effects.[31] Some of the members of this company came from the School such as Frankenhaeuser's friend, Ritva Lehtinen, participating in performances described as 'a form of total theatre that is stimulating, vital and beautiful'. Moore's dancers could also act, and he combined their talents with 'sounds that can dance and light that can do almost anything'.[32] When in 1970 *Moving Being* took its work to New York, the American theatre director and writer Charles Marowitz wrote of the company as 'the most committed attempt in England to fertilize the archaic notions of dance'.[33]

Howard's commitment to the avant garde is once again reflected in the way that he encouraged Moore to give full reign to his pioneering spirit. That pioneering spirit was to spread through the activities of the School and the Company under the guidance of Contemporary Dance Trust as the whole enterprise expanded and grew. For the younger dancers in the Company, The Place offered a tangible future for the first time. Namron, who had graduated from the small touring London Contemporary Dance Group to the main Company, took full advantage: 'when we came here, we had a two-week season in the theatre, two weeks, amazing, and we had contracts with the Company. And Robin said to us, if you want to earn some extra money, we need some teachers to work in the School. How much were we paid for giving classes – 10 shillings. So I did two classes a week.' Moving between Company and School, he summed up his view of the central protagonists of the whole adventure: 'Bob was the guru, Mop was the go-between, and Robin was the magician.'[34]

1   Email communication, 25 June 2016

2   Ibid.

3   See Clarke and Crisp 1989, p. 29

4   Dandeker later became Dandeker-Arnold and was the founder of Candoco in 1991

5   The ballet-trained Roope travelled to New York in 1964 on a Harkness Fellowship to study at the Martha Graham School. She returned to London in 1966 to teach and choreograph.

6   Interview with van Laast, April 2016

7   Interview with Eager, July 2015

8   Interview with Alston, August 2015

9   Interview with Cohan, August 2015 and Clarke and Crisp 1989, p.32

10 Clarke and Crisp 1989, p.33

11 Interview with Eager, July 2015

12 Clarke and Crisp 1989, p.46.

13 Interview with van Laast, May 2016

14 Email communication, 25 June 2016

15 Interview with Alston, August 2015

16 Interview with Eager, July 2015

17 Jordan 1992, pp.20-21

18 Ibid.

19 Jackson 2013, p.147

20 Jordan 1992, p.23

21 Clarke and Crisp 1989, p.36

22 Interview with van Laast, May 2016

23 Email correspondence, 25 June 2016

24 Clarke and Crisp 1989, p.36

25 Abridged from Jackson 2013, pp.148-149

26 Clarke and Crisp 1989, pp.46-47

27 Author's recollections and personal collection; alanherdmanpilates.co.uk/website
28 Clarke and Crisp 1989, p.33
29 Ibid.
30 Interview with Alston, August 2015
31 Jordan 1992, p.23
32 Mackrell 1992, p.17 and *Observer* review as cited in Mackrell, 1992, p.17
33 Cited in Jordan 1992, p.23
34 interview with Namron, June 2018

Chapter 5

Strong leaders and creative students – the early 1970s

The move to Euston and The Place in 1969 and the subsequent expansion represented a sea change for the LCDS students. For van Laast, it brought his dance studies into focus: 'suddenly it all clicked – I think my year at Berners Place had been a bit of a joyride and fun – a bit of a hobby. And then I became much more serious about the whole thing.' Not only were the students now able to work in a substantial building, but two new teachers were about to arrive who would lead the students in both technique and choreography for the following two decades – Jane Dudley and Nina Fonaroff. Van Laast also recognised the bonus of having the Company rehearsing in the building and performing in the theatre: 'we had fabulous classes and suddenly there was a real focus to the School. Having the Company there on hand, you could see exactly one's trajectory – if you got it right you could get into the Company. At that moment I just worshipped the Company. We had amazing characters like Bob Powell just walking around.'[1]

The School's reputation was growing, and by 1971, it had increased its intake to 63 students spread over the three years of the course.[2] The School continued to welcome visiting teachers, often from America. There was the jazz dancer Matt Mattox, memorable in the 1954 film musical *Seven Brides for Seven Brothers*, and Dudley Williams, the charismatic star of the Alvin Ailey Dance Theatre. But in 1970 the redoubtable Jane Dudley arrived, also from the United States, to take up a permanent position. She was to play a major role in formalising the dance education at LCDS, and would stay for over twenty years from 1970 to 1991, shaping more than one generation of dancers. If Cohan was the founder, she could be, and was, described as the School's 'godmother'.[3] Jane Dudley had danced with the Graham Company through the late 1930s and early 1940s, and had created the role of 'The Ancestress' in *Letter to the world* (1940). By then she had also choreographed her small-scale masterwork, the solo *Harmonica Breakdown* (1938), revived under her direction in London. Her teaching and choreography in America led her to forge strong links with the Batsheva Company in Israel, and so she brought to the School a rich seam of experience with students of widely different standards across both technical and creative areas.

With Cohan focussing more and more on the Company, the School continued its strong link with the Graham fountainhead when the post of Vice Principal and Director of Dance Studies was offered to Dudley. Her experience with the Graham Company, and beyond, paralleled that of Cohan, so he had confidence that he now had 'someone strong who knew the Graham technique inside out' but also 'someone he trusted and liked'.[4] Cohan and Dudley had taught together at Berners Place, where he had first recognised her unstoppable energy when they discussed how to manage the four week beginners classes that took place in the evenings: 'in those early times the evening classes were not that separate from the School. We thought that those classes were going to produce people for the Company and Jane thought that the course needed the best teachers, so she said, "why don't you and I share that?" I said, "what, no, I can't do that Jane," but she said "if I can do it, you can do it!" So we did do it and it was absolutely true because at the end of four weeks they looked like dancers because we were relentless with them.'[5]

Always uncompromising and forthright, Dudley was an exacting teacher and in the studio her approach and methods could seem daunting. A formidable figure in a black scooped-neck top and a long black skirt, and, because of her arthritic hips, moving with a pronounced limp, she exhorted her students in a tone that would brook no argument to 'open up and project – lift in the chest, lead with the breastbone'.[6] Sean Feldman, who was at LCDS from 1983-1986, agrees that Dudley was 'tough but she always encouraged such a sense of beauty and elegance in the movement that it lifted you up somehow. Jane and the other teachers I had as a student taught me to move from as deeply within me as I could.'[7]

The choreographer Kate Flatt, who trained first at the Royal Ballet School and joined the School as a mature student in 1973, also speaks about the 'interiority' of Dudley's approach: 'Jane wanted us to move as individuals but without any outer embellishments. Everything came from the body's centre and the organic use of the torso in the spirals we made around the spine. We had fully to extend the spine as we lifted the head – there were no half measures for Jane, everything was pushed to the limit.' Flatt also remembers Dudley's straight-talking when she was firmly instructed not to dance in the manner of the 'fancy school' she had attended.[8]

Cohan is frank about his work with Dudley in the 1970s and what did and did not work for the students: 'Jane and I tried lots of things. We tried a syllabus of exercises for different classes including material that they had to do. We wanted them to know certain basics as they were practised in the old percussive technique – the very early Graham. We thought that they should know of these and experience them at some point, but the problem was nobody else would teach them – we were the only ones because people didn't feel secure in this older technique.'[9]

Dudley was a consummate teacher of Graham technique and one who throughout her years at LCDS maintained the highest standards whether teaching technique, or in her how-to-teach sessions, or her movement classes. The resident LCDS accompanist, Judyth Knight, saw Dudley's methods close up: 'apart from the technique classes that Jane gave, she also taught a second year choreography class called Movement, which I had to play for every year. That was a kind of improvisation. She had people improvising and then she would put it together, and we would present a performance in July. That performance had a structure, it had an expression. She used to take a theme. I remember one theme was children's nursery rhymes. And people were very much encouraged to improvise. But my goodness if they were going to point their foot, their foot had to be pointed! And they'd say, "I feel", and she'd say, "don't tell me what you're feeling, let me see what you're *doing*".'[10]

Dudley describes a similar approach that she took with first-year students: 'I taught a class based on my work with Hanya Holm [exploring themes] such as a swing or breath. They would improvise by letting the quality of a swing move them. Then I would lead off on the diagonal as Hanya had done. Oftentimes I would ask them to bring in material such as a dream or a description of their room and we would work with that. All this material went into their "resource notebooks" which I think some of them still have now.'[11] Although Dudley diversified in these more creatively focused classes, the technical aspect of any form of dance training at the School was for her of paramount importance: 'we were really building up a new tradition of serious dance training and it was tough at the beginning. My position was that you can't do anything without having a proper physical training. You can't choreograph. You can't consider yourself a dancer unless you can hold your leg in the air for twenty-four counts. Students came to us without a clue about what it means to take a dance class, to submit to physical discomfort, to get tired and to work hard.'[12]

Certainly these rigorous principles coincided with Howard's ambitions. Speaking in a documentary film made about the School in 1971, he described the aims and vision of his enterprise: 'the idea is that we will first of all have good dancers and choreographers for our own company, people also for other companies.' He goes on, however, to outline his future goals – goals which at the time were prophetic but which contained the seeds of LCDT's eventual demise: 'I think it most important that I am hoping a large number of them will start up their own companies. We ought in this country to have small dance groups, in at least six places in this country. They should all be friendly competitors of ours. Only once that happens and once some of them say that we are doing things in all the wrong ways – that we are too old-fashioned – only then, I think, will we have succeeded in what we are trying to do here.'[13] Howard could hardly have predicted the explosion of small-scale dance companies that would emerge. The Arts Council listed over 100 in 1989,[14] and this would be one contributory factor in the closure of LCDT in 1994.[15]

From Howard's words in 1971, it is clear that he was trying to attain the best of both worlds – a school that trained highly proficient dancers whilst also maintaining a spirit of creative curiosity and rebellion. Dudley was a witness to some of these *jeux d'esprit*: 'I'll always remember Robin and I being invited into Studio 6 where eggs were being scrambled on a burner in the centre of the room. We were each offered a paper plate for our eggs and there were two bare-chested men in shorts, one playing the piano and another with an alarm clock around his neck. On another occasion in the theatre, a plastic sheet filled with water hung from beams in the ceiling. Later, the bag was pierced, the water spilling into a tub on the floor. There were three television sets also involved, all playing different programmes simultaneously. Some of this was very ingenious but what dancing there was I can't remember. That's because there wasn't any. Robin just loved this. It was the kind of thing he'd hoped would go on in the school. From the start the students put a great deal of energy into their own events.'[16]

Choreographic experimentation extended into the company with LCDT mounting ambitious works such as *Stages* in 1971. Cohan's first full-length work was 'a multimedia event with stunning lighting effects, changes of costume, gymnastics [and other] ingredients which appealed directly to young people,' creating new and younger audiences for contemporary dance.[17] Van Laast, a company member by 1971, who performed in *Stages*, recalled his experience at that time: 'the design was extraordinary because they turned the Place Theatre round and we performed on three different levels – totally original. In the second act we wore pop-art costumes designed by Norberto Chiesa and the choreography was groundbreaking in its athleticism – we were coached by the British Olympic gymnastics specialist and it was just as original as adding breakdancing to ballet. The audience loved it. *Stages* completely caught the zeitgeist.' Aside from his opportunity to be in the first ever performances of *Stages*, van Laast was exposed to a whole range of leading American choreographers: 'I was working with Anna Sokolow, the scariest person you've ever met; in addition we were doing Graham and Taylor works. Cunningham came and taught us class, Dan Wagoner came over and he taught and choreographed on us. So we were working with these really brilliant people – incredible pioneers of contemporary dance, the people who must have gone out there and developed it.'[18]

The varied riches of the Company's repertoire at this time were eagerly embraced by the students. The talented performers eyed the Company as a destination, while those who wanted to make dance were offered workshops and showcases. Cohan was explicit about encouraging this: 'we had workshops from the very beginning: I made a rule early on. Everybody knew that anybody at The Place: student, teacher, company member, that did a dance that I thought was good enough, could go into the rep, so people were trying.'[19] No one benefitted more from this than Richard Alston, whose *Nowhere Slowly*, a work for three dancers workshopped in 1970, was taken into the Company rep. This was the eighth piece of choreography made in his student years, and was followed shortly after he had finished the three-year course by five further dances in 1971. He broke away from Graham's expressionism, following more the inspiration of Merce Cunningham and the Judson Dance Theater Movement with their focus on non-narrative and non-theatrical elements. In *Shiftwork* from 1971 for instance two women individually walked several times around a wardrobe whilst Alston 'pace[d] out a series of squares of ever-decreasing size in a corner downstage.'[20] This creative energy led to the formation in 1972 of the first breakaway independent contemporary dance company, the collective 'Strider', which performed throughout the country till 1975.

The School also harnessed Alston's energy to help with teaching choreography and composition. His early lessons in choreography at Berners Place had been taught by the American Edith Scott, but he was firm about taking this class in a new direction: 'it had to be something that I thought up myself, which I think is what the Americans call chutzpah of the first degree really, and so there I was one year out of school teaching choreography in the school.'[21] Owing much to the post-Cunningham influence, a major factor in his own work, he 'devised a course in which the notion of dance could be expanded to include pedestrian movement and task-like activity, an extreme reaction against the highly stylised emotional gestures of the past'.[22] Other students followed Alston's experimental approach 'setting up an alternative workshop within the School'.[23] This was all a far cry from the situation that Cohan found in 1967: 'there was still the idea in this country that you had to be born a choreographer, you didn't learn, you couldn't learn. That was the ballet method, you had to know how to do it and nobody could teach you.'[24]

The School attracted other energetic and creative teachers. The dancer and choreographer Fergus Early arrived in 1971 to teach ballet and folk dance, but his portfolio was considerably wider. Stephanie Jordan writes that 'the works for students that he directed with [the composer] Michael Finnissy were notable for the manner in which performers crossed disciplines, singing, speaking and playing instruments as well as dancing.'[25] If we add to this diversity the fact that in 1971 the visiting drama tutor, John Riche, 'introduced a breadth of techniques from the new fringe theatre movement: improvisation, wordplay, trust games, circus skills, and the notion of street theatre production',[26] it is evident that LCDS students explored a full range of contemporary theatre practices. Michael Finnissy, who was to become one of the UK's leading modernist composers, continued the music classes he had begun in Berners Place, and 'identified himself with all that was innovatory at the School. Many of the alternative choreographers collaborated with him before he left in 1974.'[27]

There was an atmosphere of freedom and experiment in the air. Into this creative group of students came Sally Potter (1971-74) who would become a distinguished film director and screenwriter, and the ex-Royal Ballet dancer and independent choreographer Jacky Lansley (1971-74). The School Principal Pat Hutchinson was unfailingly behind student expression, as Alston remembered: 'about a year or two after the 1968 Paris student revolutions, the students here got rather discontented and were politically aware enough to think "we could just occupy the building, we could actually close the school for a day and discuss what we think." Sally Potter was one of them and Jacky Lansley was another. Pat said "what a marvellous idea, you should go ahead and do it" and so that's what they did. Robin was absolutely livid. But Pat was really extraordinary. I think she was a kind of Jeremy Corbyn of her day.'[28]

In 1972 into the midst of this spirit of artistic rebellion and creative anarchy came Nina Fonaroff. She would be the most influential teacher of choreography in the School for the next twenty years. A former dancer with the Graham Company, it was Dudley who recommended her for the post of Head of Choreography, and by the time that the next permanent Principal of the School was appointed, Richard Ralph, in 1979, she had fully established herself. Ralph was impressed not only by her qualities as a teacher but also by her extraordinarily rich cultural background: 'her parents were professional musicians, and she remembered as a child Jascha Heifetz, and Pablo Casals as family friends and visitors to her home. She moved in those extraordinary circles in New York, and that never left her, that sense of the highest of standards.'[29]

By the time of her appointment Fonaroff was already a highly experienced choreographer, though her career as a dancer began in 1936 when she joined Graham's all-female Group. Shortly afterwards she became Louis Horst's assistant for his classes in Pre-Classic Dance

Forms and Modern Dance Forms.[30] Cohan himself had been through the systematic choreographic course taught by Louis Horst. Horst was a formidable musician – working with many choreographers and companies, notably with Martha Graham as composer of works such as *Primitive Mysteries* (1931) and *El Penitente* (1941) and as her musical director until 1948. He taught dance composition and choreography from the late 1920s until his death in 1964, and Cohan was to bring his ideas into LCDS. Fonaroff came with the same first-hand experience: '[Horst's] practical composition classes were divided into two parts: Pre-Classic Forms [were used] as a basis for learning structure. The Modern Forms were based on the history of modern painting, modern music and modern thinking. His teaching was, among other things, a general cultural education. He inspired not only dancers, but also young actors who later became very famous and never forgot Louis.'[31]

But by the time Fonaroff arrived at LCDS she had evolved her own methods. Although she always remained indebted to Horst she now rejected his system. Despite the fact that Horst had gone some way towards 'freeing choreography from the facile pull of music,'[32] Fonaroff did not hold that musical structure could be imposed on dance: '[dance] gets there through a different energy, it gets there through a theatrical and movement "want", but not through a mathematical (system) which is in music... I think that in every art really, the content or subject matter has to make its own form.'[33] Fonaroff's classes had therefore little to do with Horst's system but concentrated on 'pulse and rhythm' rather than on choreographic content. Phillip Johnston, Fonaroff's biographer described her classes as consisting of 'a series of short movement studies, often performed in silence. Six students in the class worked on choreographic assignments each week with small groups of dancers in the studio. The class would come together at the end of the week to share the work assignments they had been creating and discuss with Nina the process of crafting the movement.'[34]

For Kate Flatt, Fonaroff was an inspirational teacher with a 'sharp, critical eye'. 'She watched carefully and instantly knew what was not working and would tell you to go away and fix it. She could identify phrases that "didn't seem to mean anything" in the context of what we were doing and was constantly advising us to pare away and rethink our work.' Flatt also found the complex rhythmic exercises that Fonaroff set for the students in pairs or groups, 'very challenging' but illuminating.[35] She also appreciated Fonaroff's ballet classes which she gave to the first and second year students. Having trained with Vera Fokine and later with Muriel Stuart at Balanchine's American School of Ballet, Fonaroff had much to offer the LCDS students: 'even though I had had a lot of ballet training, I found that I still learnt details of timing and technique from Nina'.[36]

Dudley and Fonaroff were well acquainted and respected one another but they constantly squabbled. On the one hand Dudley had expected Fonaroff to teach Horst's system and was 'infuriated' when rather than delivering Horst's tried and tested course, she spent two years 'just working things out'.[37] On the other hand, according to Flatt, they argued over space and time, always at a premium. Fonaroff wanted the students to have plenty of opportunity to develop their choreography, whereas Dudley was annoyed when this time ate into the technical training.[38]

There was one development where technical training and student choreography flowered together. From 1969 there had been a small touring group taking technique demonstration and a repertoire of dances to schools and small venues. The School supported a similar venture in 1971 and Alston was very much a part of this: 'we used to go out as a little group of students and we called ourselves Dance Workshop, and then at a certain point, Flora Cushman who was a teacher [and choreographer] from America took charge of this group'.[39] The X Group – 'X standing for Experimental'[40] – that Cushman led, gave performance experience to talented third-year students.

Apart from performing, the students had a taste of the mixed blessings of a life on tour, experienced by Anca Frankenhaeuser: 'touring in the White Lady[41] to Leeds, being lost and not able to understand the directions given by well-meaning locals', with a diet of 'chips, mushy peas and other leftovers from lunch in school halls; staying in digs of every variety but mostly of the nylon sheets and bad coffee variety. Not to mention making sure you had the right coins for the heater meter. These kinds of digs carried on into LCDT touring until we became more savvy about living away from home. It made the homecoming all the more sweet; not only our own bed and good coffee, but The Place with "our very own studios", flapjacks in the café and friendly familiar faces all around us.'[42]

Many of the X Group dancers like Frankenhaeuser graduated into the Company after performing with the Group and finishing their School course. These included Celeste Dandeker and Paula Lansley, and it was an early indication of the part that the School would play in providing Cohan with talented dancers. Later in their careers some of these dancers would extend the frontiers of contemporary dance. Dandeker, for instance, co-founded the pioneering Candoco Dance Company (1991), bringing together disabled and non-disabled dancers, and commissioning work from internationally renowned choreographers.

The Group opened its arms to one exceptional dancer, who was to become an outstanding member of the Company. Patrick Harding-

Irmer had arrived from Australia aged 27 to join evening classes at the School. Harding-Irmer did not take his first dance class until the age of 24 although his talent was notable from the outset: 'the X Group was just about to go out on tour and I replaced another male dancer. Anca pretty much taught me the works and the Graham technique demonstration and off we went the next week. I think I cheated in the technique with a great deal of integrity!'[43] Harding-Irmer bypassed the three years of the course but with the X Group received a valuable opportunity to sample the life of the professional dancer and exemplified the School's openness to spotting raw talent wherever it could.

In October 1970 the School had been recognised by the Inner London Education Authority 'for the acceptance of grant-aided students'.[44] This was a much-needed opportunity for prospective students to receive funding for their training from local education authorities; and a consolidation of the creative side was achieved in October 1974 with a further grant of £20,500 over three years from the Calouste Gulbenkian Foundation. The lion's share of this went to the establishment of a new Department of Choreography, directed by Fonaroff, and funding was awarded to Lansley and Potter for their independent Limited Dance Company. The grant also contributed to the funding of a librarian and special technical equipment for the school's workshop programme.[45]

In 1974 Hutchinson retired as the School Principal but consistency of leadership was sustained when she was temporarily replaced by Robin Howard, himself, as Director of the School, with Dudley as his deputy and Head of the Dance Department. The highly experienced ex-LCDT dancer, Clare Duncan, became Co-ordinator and Director of Student Affairs,[46] and by 1974 students had themselves organised a committee to represent their concerns. At a meeting on October 21, 1974 various matters were discussed, with Robin Howard raising the issue 'that everyone agreed was the most difficult problem in the school – the overcrowding'.[47] Clearly LCDS was thriving because 130 full-time students were enrolled for the autumn term, with 200 on part-time courses,[48] but that itself underlined the problem discussed with the students that needed to be solved – further space to expand.

1. Interview with van Laast, May 2016
2. See Jackson 2013, p.160
3. Mackrell 2000
4. Jackson 2013, p.163.
5. Interview with Cohan, August 2015
6. Author's personal recollection
7. Feldman in McKim 2004, pp.53,55
8. Interview with Flatt, February 2016
9. Interview with Cohan, August 2015
10. Interview with Knight, September 2015
11. Dudley 1999
12. Ibid.
13. Robin Howard in Anna Sokolow at The Place
14. Devlin 1989, p.52
15. Parry 1994, p.338. See also Jackson 2013, pp.296-297
16. Dudley 1999
17. Mansfield 1985, p.125
18. Interview with van Laast, May 2016; see also Anna Sokolow at The Place
19. Interview with Cohan, August 2015
20. Jordan 1992, p.28
21. Interview with Alston, August 2015
22. Jordan 1992, p.28
23. Ibid.
24. Interview with Cohan, August 2015
25. Jordan 1992, p.16
26. Ibid.

27 Jordan 1992, p.16

28 Interview with Alston, August 2015

29 Interview with Ralph, June 2015

30 Meisner 2013 and Johnston 2015, p.44

31 Johnston 2015, pp.46-47

32 Ibid.

33 In Johnston 2015, p.45

34 Johnston 2015, pp.89-90

35 Interview with Kate Flatt, February 2016; see also Johnston 2015, p.6

36 Interview with Kate Flatt, February 2016

37 In Jackson 2013, p.164. See also Johnston 2015, p.88

38 Interview with Flatt, February 2016

39 Interview with Alston, August 2015. See also Jordan 1992, p.29

40 Clark and Crisp 1989, p.57

41 The White Lady was the pet name for the white Ford Transit which covered many miles in Europe and the UK

42 Email communication, 25 June 2016

43 Ibid.

44 Clarke and Crisp 1989, p.53. See also Jackson 2013, p.164

45 Contemporary Dance Trust Press Release – New Department, New Awards for London School of Contemporary Dance, 24 October 1974, Contemporary Dance Trust Archive, V&A Museum

46 Ibid.

47 Minutes of LCDS Joint Officers Committee meeting, 21 October 1974, Contemporary Dance Trust Archive, V&A Museum

48 Contemporary Dance Trust Press Release – New Department, New Awards for London School of Contemporary Dance, 24 October 1974, Contemporary Dance Trust Archive, V&A Museum

Chapter 6

Buildings secured, crisis averted – the mid to late 1970s

On the surface students and staff were benefitting from the giant leap from the one studio beginning in Berners Place to the potential of The Place. A lease costing £10,000 per annum had been signed between CDT and UK Provident Institutions (UKPI), the freehold owners of 17 Dukes Road, to run until 1990, and the future seemed relatively secure.[1] But as early as 1972 Howard was notified of a bombshell. In the lease agreement the owners had reserved the right to redevelop the site in 1977, but on 10 August 1972 Howard received a letter insisting that 'it is the freeholders' desire to commence the redevelopment of the property and would prefer to have vacant possession in September 1974'.[2] Howard sprang into action, 'playing for time' as he put it by getting the façade of Dukes Road listed as of historic value,[3] and writing to various people in the arts world that 'The Place is being torn down for redevelopment' and soliciting their support.[4] In 1974 it appeared that Howard's strategy had worked and if he could raise the purchase price the owners would be prepared to sell the freehold to the Trust, not only of the Dukes Road site but the adjacent Oyez House on Flaxman Terrace.

Raising the necessary sum looked a formidable task until a call came from the Chairman of the Arts Council, Lord Gibson, saying that he had a potential backer in the office.[5] This was the property tycoon Gabriel Harrison and he was immediately interested. To involve him more closely it was proposed 'that he should assume Chairmanship of the Trust',[6] and with fateful irony Harrison wrote in a foreword to the Company brochure of 1974 that 'he was pleased to accept and hope that I shall be able to play my part in helping to further strengthen this remarkable organisation'.[7] Ruefully Howard wrote later that 'at one time the raising of the necessary money looked as easy as money-raising can ever be – a generous patron had offered £500,000, but he died and the Trust got nothing'.[8] This switchback ride from the heights to the depths is etched into Robert Cohan's memory: 'Gabriel said he would buy it for us and we went through all the paperwork to accept the money. He went into hospital for a minor operation and died, and when they did his finances, they found that he was broke. All his money was in buildings and property that were going to be developed. So Robin was faced with this £400,000 and that broke him.'[9]

Following Harrison's death at the end of 1974, Lord Drogheda, President of the Trust launched a £1million pound appeal as the cost of both properties was put at £650,000 and more money would be needed to fund rebuilding work.[10] But it was Howard once again who had to save the ship from going under. His beloved antique books, including 'the first four Shakespeare folios, a quarto, the first published edition of Shakespeare's poems and a very considerable collection of Elizabethan and Jacobean plays,'[11] went under the hammer as did his share of the farm partnership he managed with his brother. Following tough negotiations the original purchase price was reduced to £400,000,[12] and, finally, on 9 September 1976 the sum of £402,414.38p obtained the freehold of both buildings for the Trust.[13] The School and Company now had security and room to grow.

Despite this turbulence the School had continued as normal, and saw an increase in student numbers. To the outside world the presence of 'contemporary dance' in the world of dance education and dance theatre was making an ever greater impact. In 1973 Julyen Hamilton was an 'A' level student aiming for university, but discovered Alston's avant garde group Strider when it came to perform in Cambridge, and it changed his life: 'I stood up in the middle of the [the performance] and said "I want to do that" before realizing with embarrassment that I was in the audience.[14] I went to The Place [LCDS] and spoke to Pat Hutchinson and asked if I could get in. She said they would give it a thought; I said I was going back on the train and could she tell me now please, and luckily, dear eccentric that she was, she saw that it was heartfelt and said yes – I don't know what rules she was breaking!'[15] Hamilton went on to make a 40-year career in dance as a teacher, choreographer and dancer, performing his solo pieces internationally.[16]

Kate Flatt was another recruit who was looking for 'something different to ballet'. She joined in 1973 after friends and colleagues pointed her towards The Place: 'I wanted to feed my choreographic imagination, a career that I was beginning to pursue at that time, so they told me to come to the School.'[17] Flatt enrolled for the one-year course, then moved up a year to take the third year of the three-year course and stayed on for 'what was loosely called the fourth year'.[18] When she joined in 1973, she found herself in class with students of different ages and abilities ranging from the very young Corrinne Bougaard who went on to found Union Dance Company in 1983, to more mature students such as Craig Givens, subsequently a highly regarded theatre designer. Flatt herself became a successful choreographer working across dance theatre, film, opera and musicals including The Royal Shakespeare Company's production of *Les Misérables* in 1985. Known for her work as a movement director, she teaches movement and choreography, and is an authority on national and traditional dance.[19]

Inspired by the overall artistic and technical standards of the School, Flatt responded to the deep engagement with the Graham technique: 'there was exploration of how the impulse to move originated from the body's centre and created the impetus to shape the movement. This shaping was not a matter of assuming positions and static movement, but an organic power emanating from the torso as it moved around the spine to create energy and a strong emphasis on the play between the muscles in the upper back and shoulder area that we call épaulement. The atmosphere of striving for the very best reflected Graham's philosophy and her achievement. It was high art and representative of the American abstract expressionists, bringing with it a seriousness of purpose, technical rigour and artistic authenticity.'[20]

Flatt came into contact with teachers who were, like the redoubtable Dudley, close to Graham. Cohan, Noemi Lapsezon and Juliet Fisher had inherited Graham's dedication and held high expectations of the students. Other teachers were drawn from the Company – Linda Gibbs, Robert North, Ross McKim and Clare Duncan – all of whom had engaged deeply with Cohan's Graham-inspired technique: 'above all, teachers such as Dudley wanted to see the movement coming from the individual and performed from an authentic place within that individual'.[21]

The reputation of the Company and the School was widened in the mid-1970s when Cohan devoted energy and commitment to setting up Residencies. These took the message of contemporary dance around the country to schools, colleges and community centres. Beginning in 1976 in Yorkshire and Humberside, LCDT shared their work with teachers, students and children, even to the extent that Cohan choreographed *Khamsin* in front of them.[22] Students and pupils from a range of educational backgrounds benefitted from the experience of direct contact with members of the Company, and the Company dancers stayed within the college for a period of seven days or more with a programme of basic classes and demonstrations of repertoire, culminating in a performance.

One future dancer who experienced the first residencies in 1976 was Dharshan Singh Buller: 'the first time I saw Bob (Cohan), I was 13 years old. He had a 'perm', was wearing a black leather jacket and platform boots and sunglasses on a cloudy day in Leeds. He came to watch an LCDT residency at my school in Leeds; my first contact with the world of professional dance.' LCDT's residencies continued throughout the 1980s, recruiting talented youngsters to the School like Singh Bhuller: 'as a product of the LCDT residencies, I can now see that Bob had the capacity to look at the bigger picture. He was able to engage young dancers and attract a wider audience.'[23] Singh Bhuller, as well as choreographing work for Rambert and his own company, became artistic director of Phoenix Dance Theatre from 2002 to 2006.[24]

After Pat Hutchinson retired and Howard's interregnum ended in 1975, Travis Kemp was appointed as Principal and stayed till 1979. Kemp had danced with many early British ballet companies including Ninette de Valois' Vic-Wells Ballet, Ballet Rambert, Anna Pavlova's Company, and the Markova-Dolin Company. Together with his wife, Molly Lake, he formed what became known as the Continental Ballet, but in 1954 he accepted de Valois' invitation to teach and direct the Turkish National Ballet School, introducing it to his and Molly Lake's Cecchetti-inspired methods. Although his career was grounded in ballet teaching and performance, like Pat Hutchinson before him, his experience of running a school made him a trusted choice to become principal of LCDS.

Kemp may have managed the School, but for Alston it was Molly Lake who made a lasting impression: 'she was one of the great Cecchetti ballet teachers. She was already in her 80s and quite eccentric, but her classes at the end of her life were wonderful.' Jane Dudley remained Head of Contemporary Dance and Alston recognised her as 'the artistic head of the school, while Travis was really the administrator who walked around in cavalry twill trousers and a check shirt looking as though he'd dropped out of the army. It was Jane who organised everything artistic and invited the choreographers in.'[25]

Peter Connell, who joined the staff as a ballet teacher in 1976, remembers the latter 1970s as an 'interesting but chaotic time, because we were trying to use the studios while they were banging walls through'. Work was planned at The Place 'to refurbish the theatre and restaurant and the reconditioning of existing changing facilities',[26] and by September 1979, building work in the new school premises in Flaxman Terrace was also underway. By the beginning of that school year, it offered 'three new dance studios, two music rooms, the body control studio, changing rooms and workshops',[27] all ready and open for business, and by September 1980, a fourth studio and offices for the Trust and School. But it was one step up and two steps back for Peter Connell: 'we got Flaxman Terrace which was a great relief as it gave us much more space. The downside was that in order to redress some of the shortfall in funding, Robin invited the Rambert School in. Going from a cramped existence into a palatial existence didn't last very long, because Rambert took two of the studios full-time, and that was back to square one again.'[28]

Peter Connell's frustration, shared by the teaching staff, at losing valuable space was prompted by urgent financial need, as the draft of the Annual Report to Governors and Members of the Contemporary

Dance Trust for 1979/1980, makes clear. The offer to give a home to the Rambert School of Ballet from September 1979 for 'up to two years' was an example of Howard's friendship with Dame Marie Rambert, but it also ensured 'an almost guaranteed income'.[29] Further comings and goings at The Place included the establishment of the Central School of Ballet in 1982 founded by Ann Stannard and Christopher Gable. Central stayed there until it moved to permanent premises at Herbal Hill in Clerkenwell, East London, in 1986.

Kenneth Olumuyiwa Tharp came to the School in 1978, then joined LCDT, returning in 2007 to the post of Chief Executive of CDT. He found sharing studios with Central enlightening: 'we were quite separate, we didn't really do anything together but we were nosey and we looked through the windows into the studio – I have an abiding memory of looking through what was then studio 5, which is now a lecture room, and which from my memory was narrow and long with a low ceiling and once upon a time might have been the rifle range. I remember us constantly looking through that studio and seeing a particular male teacher who seemed to terrorise the young men – they'd be standing there on relevé for what seemed like an eternity, shaking whilst being shouted at, and us thinking, well, thank goodness that's not us!'

Tharp found that the pressure on space for actual LCDS students meant they had to find any corner to meet and swap ideas: 'there was a small student common room as you enter what is now the back entrance to the theatre – a little hide-away which no longer exists. There were so few places to go. The students sat around on the steps – there was a real sense of hippiness but one that reverberated with a vibe and an energy which was very present. You walked down the stairs through people to get to where you were going, and for the café you climbed up the stairs to the macrobiotic restaurant which you paid for with red and yellow tokens. Woe betide you if you got to the top of the steps and hadn't bought your tokens with you – you faced a difficult call as to whether or not you were going to go all the way down the steps, back along the corridor, find the place to buy them, come back, haul yourself up the stairs again, probably have five minutes to gulp your lunch and then get ready for your next class.'[30]

Sacrificing hard-won extra space was very hard for the LCDS dance faculty but the teachers and dancers were not the only occupants to suffer from these constraints. When Richard Ralph took up his post as Principal in 1979, he also felt the lack of suitable accommodation: 'I wasn't given an office at first. I was told on day one, here you are, this is the school office, people coming in and out, two secretaries, a little space over there, but no office. It took me my first few weeks to persuade Jack Norton, who was then director of administration and finance, to give me what was a concrete, windowless bunker at the back of the theatre in those days. I don't think it had any light, all artificial light. It was a small box, with a concrete floor, and I moved in a filing cabinet, a desk and two chairs.'[31]

The premises also failed to impress a student who arrived in 1980. This was the ballet-trained Isabel Tamen from Lisbon in Portugal. She was attracted by the recommendation of her teacher, Vasco Vallenkamp, to study at LCDS, and was avid to hone her skills in contemporary dance: 'in terms of facilities and studio spaces at LCDS, they did not compare very favourably with the Gulbenkian studios where I was brought up because that was such a modern building with very good and well-lit changing rooms. When I saw the changing rooms here, cockroaches on the floor – it was not the building that impressed me, it was more what was going on inside it.'[32]

If the facilities at LCDS were not up to scratch, there was plenty to keep the students occupied and challenged. Tharp found the curriculum rich and varied: 'looking here at the timetable, you can see that each day starts with Graham and ballet. We had Jane Dudley and Noemi Lapsezon for Graham, and Peter Connell and Molly Lake for ballet. Other subjects were music, often taught by the percussionist Peter Kehlior, choreography, choral, national dance with Kate Flatt, movement class with Jane Dudley, historical dance with Belinda Quirey, stagecraft, but there was hardly anything there that was academic.'[33]

Pernille Charrington, who joined the School in 1978 at the tender age of 15, after having already completed Easter and Summer courses at The Place, was also impressed by the range of teachers. She was taught by Cohan and by members of LCDT such as Jayne Lee, Linda Gibbs, Robert North and Anthony van Laast. She also had Fonaroff for ballet, Alan Herdman for body conditioning and remembered with particular vividness her classes with the historical dance specialist, Belinda Quirey: 'Belinda taught a completely different way of moving because of the historical dance technique which we had to acquire in order to have the ability to do her early Renaissance work. You needed a completely different transfer of weight in the body. When you are so Graham-trained to suddenly let go of that and fall into this quality of historical dance that Belinda could teach us was at times very difficult.'[34]

For Charrington, who went on to dance with English Dance Theatre and then developed a career in teaching, her choreographic work with Fonaroff and Ingegerd Lonnroth was also intense: 'Nina's classes were very demanding – you had to create something "snap" on the spot. She would say, "you go to that corner, you go to the other corner, make it in twos, in threes, I'll give you two minutes to figure it out, then show me." Then you had to adapt to the music, or work in silence. She didn't expect you to use classroom vocabulary but wanted you to discover organically where you were coming from.'[35] Notes on Charrington's composition classes with Lonnroth show the idea of using 'steps' for choreography was replaced by broader movement exploration. For example, Lonnroth asked them to note 'ten ways of resisting gravity in everyday life' including 'breathing, turning on a switch, pulling sellotape, opening a door, stirring a drink'. They had to select four of these ordinary actions and 'transform them into dance movement' ensuring that it was possible to 'see the muscle movement instead of just acting'. These movements were to be executed 'in a constant flow of normal speed, fast, slow, and with complete stillness at times'.[36]

Performance experience came in the form of termly 'sharings' when students demonstrated their work for friends, family and the rest of the school, and more importantly, the formal graduation performances at the end of the academic year. For Richard Alston, 1979 was one that was very special in the annals of the School: 'I used to come in as a guest choreographer, particularly for the graduation shows. 1979 was a phenomenal year – there have always been these years through the progress of the school where there's a sudden extraordinary chemical mix and in 1979, I made *Dumka* to music by Dvorak which included Dharshan Singh Bhuller, Kenneth Tharp, Jonathan Lunn, Pernille Charrington, Gurmit Hukam, Lauren Potter, and Jeremy Nelson.'[37]

Despite the customary crises over finance, the constant rebuilding and the sharing of the premises with other organisations, by the end of the 1970s the School was the fulcrum of the contemporary dance movement in the UK and that message was being spread through residencies, workshops and the Company. Contemporary Dance Trust had secured the freeholds of both The Place and Flaxman Terrace, so, when funds permitted, expansion would be possible, and Robin Howard's vision of a place full of creativity and ambition, a place where dancers of all ages and standards could take a full-time course, or just come to children's or evening classes, had been established. The 1980s would inevitably demand more effort and more money, but there was a solid reputation achieved during its first formative years on which to build; and a new Principal, Richard Ralph, had arrived, who was to revolutionise the teaching and create an academically-based faculty.

1   Letter dated 9 August 1968 from B.G. Shepherd & Partners to Messrs. Radcliffe & Co. Contemporary Dance Trust Archive, V&A Museum.

2   Letter from Ernest Owers & Williams, surveyors, valuers, auctioneers and estate agents, dated 10 August 1972. Contemporary Dance Trust archive, V&A Museum.

3   Clarke and Crisp 1989, p.81

4   Letter to Peter Brook and others dated 9 April 1973. Contemporary Dance Trust Archive, V&A Museum.

5   Clarke and Crisp 1989, p.81

6   Howard quoted in Clarke and Crisp 1989, p.81

7   LCDT brochure 1974, property of Pernille Charrington

8   The Place – its renovation and extension – communication from Howard 20 September 1977. Contemporary Dance Trust Archive, V&A Museum.

9   Interview with Cohan, August 2015

10 Clarke and Crisp 1989, p.95

11 Clarke and Crisp, 1989 p.17

12 Letter of 7 July 1976 from W. Theodore Richardson, Property Consultant. Contemporary Dance Trust Archive, V&A Museum.

13 Letter from Harbottle and Lewis Solicitors 9 September 1976. Contemporary Dance Trust archive, V&A Museum.

14 Hamilton 2011, p.61

15 Ibid. p.62

16 julyenhamilton.com

17 Interview with Flatt, February 2016

18 Ibid.

19 kateflatt.com

20 Interview with Flatt, February 2016

21 Ibid.

22 See Clarke and Crisp 1989, pp.105

23 Anon 2006, Singh Bhuller 2004, p.151

24 Darshan Singh Bhuller went on to add filmmaking to his career as a choreographer

25 Interview with Alston, August 2015

26 Letter to patrons from Jack Norton, 27 May 1980. Contemporary Dance Trust Archive, V&A Museum.

27 Ibid.

28 Interview with Connell, September 2015

29 Draft of the Annual Report to the Governors and Members of the CDT 1979/1980. Contemporary Dance Trust Archive, V&A Museum.

30 Interview with Tharp, July 2015

31 Interview with Ralph, June 2015

32 Interview with Tamen, July 2015

33 Interview with Tharp, July 2015

34 Interview with Charrington, January 2015

35 Ibid.

36 Charrington's notes on her composition class with Lonnroth, 5 October 1977

37 Interview with Alston, August 2015. The graduating students referred to by Alston were already emerging talents and went on to successful careers as teachers, dancers and choreographers

Chapter 7

A new principal and a piece of paper – the early 1980s

Robin Howard had become aware by the end of the 1970s that the School was in need of new energy and leadership. He also realised more than ever that the School should offer a proper academic qualification. In the late 1970s, the three-year course offered a broad-based theatrical education including technical, creative, musical, stagecraft, historical dance, body conditioning and the spiritually grounding Tai Chi. But the certificates that were awarded to full-time students on successful completion of the three-year course, were not valid in the academic marketplace.

The early days of the School provided a line to the Company and other opportunities, and so the idea of having a 'proper' qualification felt unnecessary. Van Laast, in the late 1960s and early 1970s, considered the lack was compensated for by the opportunity to teach: 'I began towards the end of my third year. You started with evening classes and then you worked your way up from that.' And his time in the Company provided him with insights which the School could not equal: 'the great thing that Bob did was that he taught us to teach. He would watch class, especially when we were teaching on the road, and he'd nudge you in one direction or another direction. We were taught that being a teacher was a really good thing to be.' The piece of paper that he received from the School on finishing his course, however, 'meant nothing'.[1]

Both Howard and Eager knew that their dancers were finding themselves at a serious disadvantage when, for instance, their time with the Company came to an end and they wanted to develop their careers beyond performance. As Eager said: 'we had these very talented professional dancers who had years of experience but they couldn't get teaching jobs.' It was clear that a recognised qualification had become vital. 'Someone like Clare Duncan for instance found it hard to teach in America. Robin had tried desperately to set up a degree programme on his own and with the help of various people, but nobody had the solid academic expertise or experience to make it happen.'[2]

With the aim of establishing a new qualification in mind, the next era of the School began with a phone call made one morning in 1978 to a 27-year-old research scholar at Oxford University. On the receiving end was Richard Ralph, converting his doctoral thesis into a book, and also teaching at Oxford's Trinity College. On the other end was Robin Howard, who in typical forthright manner opened the conversation by saying 'this phone call may take seven minutes or seven years'.[3] Howard was underestimating – the call took longer than seven minutes and Richard Ralph's future was signed up for the next 17 years.

The connection to Richard Ralph came through the music and dance critic Andrew Porter, a friend of Howard's who had supervised Ralph's doctorate on the 18th century English dancing master John Weaver some years before, when he was a Visiting Fellow at All Souls (1972-3). He knew of Ralph's wider interest in ballet and dance, ranging from the Royal Ballet to London Contemporary Dance Theatre, and there was one other timely coincidence: 'when Robin rang me, I had recently seen the Martha Graham season at the Royal Opera House, with Miss Graham's extraordinary front of curtain speech at the end of it, and I was able to say quite honestly that I adored the work of many of the artists connected to CDT, not only Bob but Sue Davies, and I remembered a wonderful performance of Strider at the Museum of Modern Art at Oxford so I had quite a bit of background, which I hadn't realised, in contemporary dance, and was certainly interested enough to respond to his invitation to come and talk about it.'

'It' was both the job of Principal and the pressing need to establish a degree course at the School. Robin Howard had already been in touch with the Council for National Academic Awards, the body which authorised degrees at many institutions outside universities, but the CNAA's initial report suggested changes needed to be made in the curriculum, and in the end, as Richard Ralph said: 'we realised that what the CNAA were looking for was not compatible with what we wanted to offer. At every turn it proved to be very difficult for us to make any progress with the CNAA.'[4]

Kate Flatt, who was teaching national dance at LCDS at the time, remembers a visit by the CNAA and meeting the distinguished ethnomusicologist and social anthropologist, Professor John Blacking: 'Professor Blacking grilled me about the authenticity of my teaching. I was able to assure him that I had studied Greek dance in Greece with a Greek-speaking anthropologist to assist me. Belinda Quirey who taught historical dance wasn't prepared to take him seriously and when he asked why nobody ever read any books at the school, she replied that there were "cartfuls of bad books about dance" and what we did at the School was to get on and actually dance. When he pointed out that as anthropologists they studied books, she asked him "well, do you dance?"'[5] It became self-evident there was no way forward with the CNAA, as Ralph made clear: 'the dance critic and academic, Peter Brinson, was a member of the panel, and they insisted on things which we didn't consider compatible with the training of a professional dancer, far too heavy on the academic side and related areas. We just felt they weren't responsive in the way that we would need them to be.'[6]

It was to the University of Kent that Ralph then turned: 'I had been an external examiner for a while at a college in Kent – and one of the people there, Chris Challis, said wouldn't it be wonderful if you went to the University of Kent for validation. So I pursued that, and as far as I'm aware we acquired the first university-validated dance degree for professional dancers in Europe, through the link with Kent.[7] With Kent we had a free rein as to what we thought was relevant to the needs of a professional dancer, because they didn't have a dance course, which was a great advantage to a dance organisation. They allowed us to say *these* are the dance standards, *these* are the requirements – and to have them monitored for the university by qualified external examiners. And they would put in quality assurance and interest in other areas which we thought were relevant on the contextual side. Although they were prepared to let us have our head they weren't a pushover by any means. They were highly intelligent people, they needed to be convinced that what we had in mind was going to work, and was going to produce what they needed and what we needed, in order to validate it.'[8]

Peter Connell who was appointed as LCDS Assistant Principal in 1987 was also involved in the negotiation: 'one of the arguments we put to the academics of Kent was that you could see a technique class as similar to somebody being given an essay subject, going to a library, researching it and writing about it. In other words, the students in class have a resource in front of them who gives them the information that they need to understand how that information can be applied to their own physical development, how to assimilate that information and to develop that material specifically for them, enabling them to make progress.'[9]

LCDS was to embark on a journey into relatively uncharted territory – integrating the hours of practice in the dance studio and on stage with scaling the lofty heights of academe. Ralph describes the situation he inherited in 1979 as 'very rough and ready. The artistic side was always pre-eminent, world-class even, but the back-up, administration, support, the curriculum, the documentation, the procedures – all needed attention.' His appointment of Iris Tomlinson[10] as his PA and School Administrator, was important to the professionalisation of this area of work. As Principal he was 'in overall charge of the School', with Jane Dudley as Director of Contemporary Dance Studies and Nina Fonaroff as Director of Choreography. Although the Principal was in charge and ultimately responsible for the whole School, 'it was only common sense to allow Dudley to get on with the artistic side of it, and Fonaroff with the

25. Nina Fonaroff, Head of Choreography from 1972 to 1991, with LCDS students of the London at The Place in 1985. Photo © Dee Conway/Bridgeman Images

26. The choreographer Viola Farber, former dancer with Merce Cunningham's company, teaching LCDS students c. 1984. Photo Anthony Crickmay. Camera Press, London

27. Robert Cohan with Kenneth Olumuyiwa Tharp and Sue Booker in the 1980s. Photograph by Anthony Crickmay, © V&A Images/Victoria and Albert Museum, London

28. Juliet Fisher in class with LCDS students in 1985. Photo © Dee Conway/Bridgeman Images.

29. The Three Degrees. Receiving their BA Honours degrees at the University of Kent in 1985, lt. to rt. Charlotte Kirkpatrick, Patrick Harding-Irmer, Anca Frankenhaeuser. LCDS archive. Photo © Ray Newsam

30. Robert Cohan's *Stabat Mater* was performed by LCDS students at Southwark Cathedral in 1983, and was also staged in Canterbury Cathedral to mark the first graduation ceremony in 1985. LCDS archive. Photo © Doris Haslehurst

31. Richard Ralph, Principal of LCDS from 1979 to 1996. Photo © Dee Conway/Bridgeman Images.

32. (left) Judyth Knight, Chief Accompanist at the School from 1966 to 1997. Photo © Leslie E.Spatt

33. (right) Susan McGuire, Head of Contemporary Dance Studies from 1991 to 1998. Photo: courtesy Susan McGuire

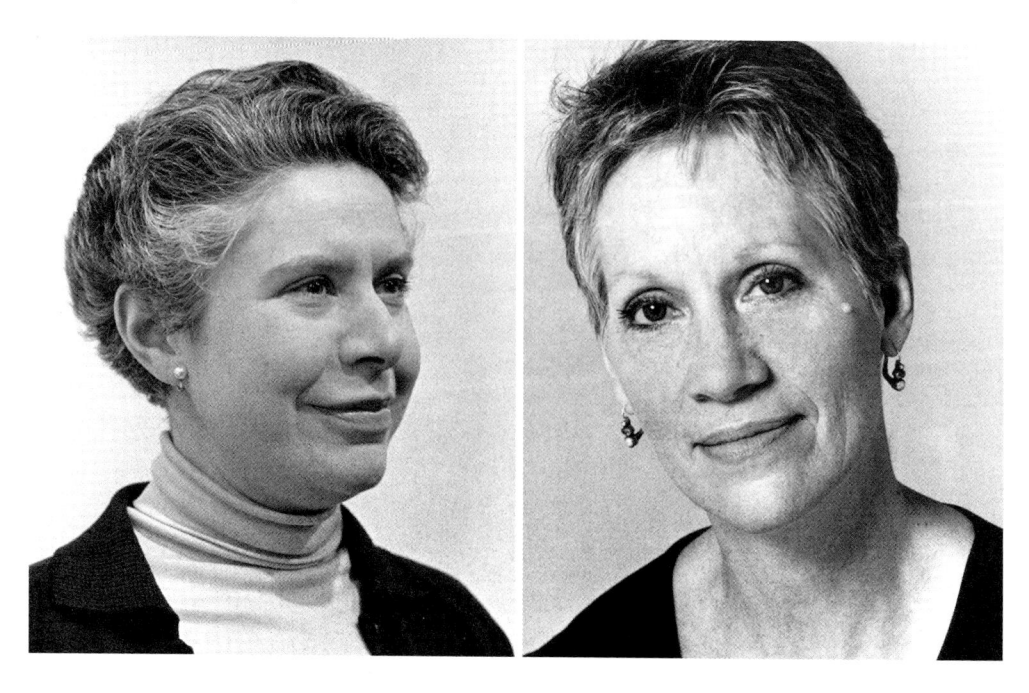

34. Photograph by Anthony Crickmay, Camera Press, London

Airborne dancers: Jane Dudley and Susan McGuire send students Paul Liburd and Henri Oguike into flight in the 1990s, and Kenneth Olumuyiwa Tharp soars in Dharshan Singh Bhuller's *The Smouldering Suit* in 1988.

35. Photograph by Bill Cooper/ArenaPAL

36. The new glass-fronted entrance to the School opened in 2001. The old entrance is the white double door on the left. Photo © Dennis Gilbert/VIEW

37. (left) The first entrance to the School on Flaxman Terrace. LCDS archive.

38. (right) The curve of the Robert Cohan studio built above the original LCDS premises. Photo © Bannerman

39. Incoming Principal of the School Veronica Lewis with Assistant Principal Peter Connell in September 1998. Photo © Catherine Ashmore

40. Students in the 'stretching zone' above the new entrance. Photo © Hugo Glendinning

41. Photo © Dee Conway/Bridgeman Images

Two contrasting performances by LCDS students: Doris Humphrey's *The Shakers* from 1931, restaged by Ernestine Stodelle in July 1985. Crystal Pite's *Polaris* in 2014 at Sadlers Wells with students from LCDS and Central School of Ballet.

42. Photo © Bill Cooper /ArenaPAL

43. The School has embraced alternative ways of gaining knowledge and awareness through the body. Pytt Geddes taught Tai Chi at LCDS from 1970 to 1996. Photograph with kind permission of her daughter Harriet Devlin

44. Chisato Ohno began teaching Gaga, the improvised exploration of movement developed by Ohad Naharin in the 1990s and joined the LCDS faculty in 2013. Photo © Matteo Carratoni

45. Richard Alston in 2014. One of the first full-time students in 1967, Alston continued his close association with The Place and the School, as teacher, choreographer, and Artistic Director of CDT and his own Company. He was knighted in 2019. Photo © Hugo Glendinning

46. Veronica Lewis, Principal of the School from 1998 to 2018, speaking at a graduation ceremony in July 2017. Photo © Alicia Clarke

47. Martin Lawrance, on the right, graduated from the School in 1993, rehearsing Liam Riddick in 2010. Photo © Hugo Glendinning

48. Rick Nodine, teacher of Contact Improvisation at LCDS from 2001, performing his Place Prize work *Dead Gig* in 2012. Photo © Benedict Johnson

49. James Cousins formed his own company in 2014, after graduating from the School. He teaches and choreographs internationally, pictured here with Ballet Nacional Chileno in 2013. Photography © Josefina Perez

50. Clare Connor, a former graduate of the School was appointed Chief Executive of CDT and Interim Principal of the School in 2017. Photo © Hugo Glendinning

choreographic side, so my role was to make it all work and hang together, to give Jane and Nina the support and the facilities and the resources that they required.'[11]

Ralph was very conscious of the School's relationship with the Company and on arriving in 1979 advocated that the School 'should take fuller advantage of the Company than we have done hitherto because it wasn't just a dance school, it was also a wonderful Company and an outstanding theatre organisation and an outreach company, so we had to take our place in that, and to ensure that we were providing dancers for Bob Cohan who at that time was recruiting exclusively from the School'.[12] Crucially, though, Ralph had to secure the degree: 'I was appointed in 1979 officially and the degree course started in 1982 so it took me three years. I remember meeting Bob in the corridor and was surprised to hear him say – "I thought you were supposed to be getting us a degree course." Clearly he found it hard to appreciate that these things take time!'[13]

From 1979, Ralph prepared for the degree by introducing appropriate theory and practice. LCDS would be 'validated as an Institution offering an undergraduate honours degree in the summer term of 1982', but he reassured the faculty and students that 'nothing that is good at present will be lost and that no bogus academic subjects will be superimposed just to please the panel'.[14] Ralph's words appear to reflect the fact that in 1979 an academically grounded degree was not popular with the faculty. The emphasis at LCDS was on the excellence of performance and choreography, and in these very early days, there was resentment towards any time and attention diverted from working towards the highest level of achievement in the studio.

Dudley summed up the concern felt by leading members of the faculty: 'I felt that an academic attitude is not the same as a dance artist's attitude. [The academic attitude] over-intellectualises and does not always help to make better dancers. More important by far is the connection to that part of oneself that makes movement and thinks in terms of dance movement and dance ideas and feelings. I felt that our aim was to teach dancers how to handle movement with their bodies.'[15] Ralph's work on the degree was inevitably taking the School in a new direction, and Dudley and others were unsure of the benefits.

But Ralph persisted, and in 1982 first the School changed its name from the London School of Contemporary Dance to the snappier London Contemporary Dance School, and secondly, in September, it launched 'an Honours Degree in Contemporary Dance validated by the University of Kent'.[16] The three-year Certificate was still offered to students, but the new, improved, qualification was at last available. It was a leap in the dark for both Howard and Ralph: 'I'd never cease to be grateful to Robin for putting his trust in a 27-year-old untried researcher from Oxford as he did. That takes courage which he had in spades of course. It wasn't necessarily easy for him to allow someone else to run what, I always thought to him, was the part in which he took the closest interest. He had a particular fondness or feeling for what the School was doing and particularly its potential.'[17]

At last LCDS would be able to provide prospective professional contemporary dancers with the opportunity to obtain that vital qualification through the 'practical and professional training in contemporary dance for which the school was internationally respected'.[18] As planned by Ralph the BA course was designed to take three years to achieve: '70% of the marks were on Dance, on Dance Practice in the studio, and Choreography. 30% was to be allocated to contextual studies. In the early days of the course there was Practical Musicianship but this was modified later. Other subjects followed courses that the students were already taking but in a more "codified" format, such as Wardrobe with Jenny Henry and Stage Design with Peter Mumford, a wonderful experience for students. There was Music, of course, then they'd have Dance History, and that would have been done practically.'[19] There were classes in poetry with John Wain, television studies with Chris Dunkley, and art and cultural studies with Chris Frayling, for which students had to go to the Royal College of Art.

Written assignments were kept to a minimum: 'although there was always some writing, even in subjects like Wardrobe, the focus was on experiential learning in the studio. That was the main impetus. It was a course that someone who wanted to be a professional dancer could do, and the extra demands of the degree work wouldn't diminish in any way their professional training or experience. The whole idea was that it would enhance it, because these were disciplines relevant to their career.'[20]

The validation document of January 1982 stipulates that from its very earliest inception the degree was to give a central place to dance performance, and aimed, as one might argue it continues to do, 'to provide a dance-education and not just a training in unrelated skills'. There was to be 'due weight' apportioned to the analytical and theoretical 'study of dance and associated subjects', which constituted Part 1, whilst Part 2 concerned technique, performance and choreography. However, the Honours element in this degree was to depend mainly on the students' abilities in Part 2 'to bring the different elements of the course into a high level of creative dance-performance'.[21]

According to Margaret Dunn's External Examiner's report on the first year of the course, there were three male and three female students[22] undertaking a programme whose aim was to 'train professional dancers with the educational and intellectual "back-up" for an honours degree'.[23] Dunn's report stated that the students' written answers and comments on subjects such as drama and television studies, anatomy, theatrical costume and design had reached 'a satisfactory standard'. But a gentle rap on the knuckles was delivered as the examiners found that the students' writing was too dependent on lecture notes and called for 'more of a balance between what has been learnt and personal comment and analysis of the material'.[24] The examiners concluded that 'a degree so originally conceived and with so few precedents in support has got off to a most satisfactory start'.[25]

What is not evident from her report is the fact that three members of LCDT also embarked in 1982 on the degree programme: Anca Frankenhaeuser, Charlotte Kirkpatrick and Patrick Harding-Irmer, bringing the first cohort up to a total of nine. Her report states that the syllabus of the LCDS students comprised three hours of dancing each day divided between Graham-based contemporary technique and ballet, with the afternoons devoted to 'contextual and supportive studies'.[26]

The three LCDT dancers had a different schedule working around their rehearsals and performances. Patrick Harding-Irmer had already been a leading Company dancer for ten years when the BA was introduced and welcomed the new challenge: 'I think we were ready for a challenge that had to do with what was most important in our lives. The thought of having to come to grips with knowledge that related directly to our careers, in fact all things that we really should know about anyway, was very compelling. It was an incredibly stimulating time. Rehearsing and performing and steeping ourselves in the studies full time was wonderful. Out on tour certain lecturers came to us, and they also sometimes brought with them cassette tapes of lectures we had missed. Plugging ourselves into the tapes until late at night with a pen and an Indian takeaway! Fortunately company class was only at midday.'[27]

Frankenhaeuser found that the chance to gain insight into performance-related subjects was very exciting: 'we had Bob Cohan monitoring our Dance Technique and Performance, Belinda Quirey on Historical and Baroque Dance, Jenny Henry on Wardrobe and Pattern Cutting, as well as studies on Human Biology and Anatomy, History of Theatre, Music Theory, stage lighting and visuals and learning the guitar! I don't think that my essay writing was very good. I loved doing the research and tended to put in too much fact instead of critical thought. I recall that my Human Biology essay and presentation was about the Digestive System, which particularly interested me because as a dancer you do need to have one that works well, and as dancers we need to think about *what* we eat, and even more so about *when* we eat.'[28]

To mark the graduation of the first students in 1985 there was a performance in Canterbury Cathedral, which for Frankenhaeuser was one of the high points of the whole process: 'Charlotte did the main part in Cohan's *Stabat Mater* (1975) with LCDS students, and Patrick and I did Jesus & Mary respectively in Robert North's *The Annunciation* (1979). It certainly was a very special treat to perform in such a special place.'[29] The actual degree ceremony followed three days later, and was an event Harding-Irmer remembers vividly: 'the ceremony itself was wonderful. My mum had come from Sydney and my aunt from Paris to be there. Anca, Charlotte and I had lovely photos taken together as "The Three Degrees" and that photo became our Christmas card for that year. Bob was always very encouraging of our academic pursuit and I think many of the dancers envied us that we had that special focus on top of our dancing. We were of course very proud to have gained our degrees with Honours Class 1... I think our technique marks were pretty good!'[30]

Another of the Company dancers who realised the advantages of gaining a degree was Kenneth Olumuyiwa Tharp who together with Christopher Bannerman and Michael Small became the second and last cohort of LCDT dancers to graduate in 1987. From then on only students at the School embarked on the degree. Tharp has a clear idea as to why he took on the challenges of such a project while with the Company: 'as a very young man, I was very determined that I wasn't going to postpone coming to train as a dancer, but when the degree became available at LCDS and also to members of LCDT, I thought that maybe it would be useful for me later on to have a degree qualification, and I was curious. I managed to get funding from the dancers' resettlement fund (now called the redevelopment fund) which financed my degree course.'

But Tharp had to integrate his studies with a busy touring schedule and the demands of working in a professional dance company: 'it was quite tough fitting our studies in with touring. Mondays were sometimes off and we would be in the School for lectures. Often when we finished a performance we had to decide whether to go out and have something to eat, or go home, have a picnic supper and work late, or just go to bed and get up early to work. There was quite a bit of writing, and we had to do a dissertation. I did mine on an aspect of ageing but it was also to do with transcendental meditation and its effect on the ageing process. We also had to study anatomy and physiology and music. There was quite a lot of essay-writing and having not done any writing since my A levels it felt a bit like being back at school again.'[31] Tharp went on to have a long and successful career with LCDT, and was there when the Company was disbanded in 1994. The 'piece of paper' that Howard and Eager had long wanted to offer the dancers and students was at last a reality.

1   Interview with van Laast, May 2016

2   Interview with Eager, July 2015

3   Howard cited in Interview with Ralph, June 2015

4   Interview with Ralph, June 2015

5   Interview with Flatt, February 2016

6   Interview with Ralph, June 2015

7   Trinity Laban achieved validation of their three-year BA Hons Dance Theatre by the Council for National Academic Awards (CNAA) in 1977 which nevertheless leaves LCDS as the first conservatoire in Europe to achieve a university-validated degree for professional dancers.

8   Interview with Ralph, June 2015

9   Interview with Connell, September 2015

10   Tomlinson, a specialist in Graham-based contemporary dance, assisted Jane Dudley with her work developing the art of teaching from 1978 to 1999

11   Ibid.

12   Interview with Ralph, June 2015

13   Ibid.

14   Ralph's mission statement, 'From the Principal to the Faculty' undated 1979, Contemporary Dance Trust Archive, V&A Museum.

15   Dudley 1999. Author's personal collection

16   Mansfield 1985, pp. 111,136. See also Ralph, R, (1988) 'An Honours Degree for Professional Dancers: Some Personal Reflections on the LCDS BA Course', *The Dancing Times*, 78, 928, pp.333-335.

17   Interview with Ralph, June 2015

18   Mansfield 1985, p.136

19   Interview with Ralph, June 2015

20   Ibid.

21   London School of Contemporary Dance, BA (Honours) Degree in Contemporary Dance for Validation by the University of Kent at Canterbury, January 1982, Contemporary Dance Trust Archive, V&A Museum.

22   Degrees were awarded to LCDS students in 1985 to Alison Duthie, Susan Haylett, Ron

Howell, David Green, Winifred Jamieson and Marek Wasniewski, Contemporary Dance Trust Archive, V&A Museum.

23 External Examiners' report on Hons. BA in Contemporary Dance at the London School of Contemporary Dance, (circa early to mid 1980s), Contemporary Dance Trust Archive, V&A Museum

24 Ibid.

25 Ibid.

26 Ibid.

27 Email communication, 25 June 2016

28 Ibid.

29 Ibid.

30 Ibid.

31 Interview with Tharp, July 2015

Chapter 8

The Graham connection loosens: changes and departures – the mid to late 1980s

In 1980 Martha Graham ceased her patronage of the School. This had been planned for and expected, but it indicated that the Graham influence was being challenged on many fronts. Howard had said that Graham had agreed to the teaching of her technique at LCDS on the basis that 'she hoped and expected that within ten years or at the most twenty years, what we were teaching would have developed in our own way and would be different from what she was teaching in her school'.[1] Howard had imported the Graham technique in the 1960s because he considered it to be 'the first of the modern techniques to be very carefully worked out and analysed and developed as a technique which you can pass on to other people'. But he was well aware that 'once you have reached a certain stage, other forms of training in modern work may be more useful',[2] and 'in what Robert Cohan is now teaching to the Company, there is something which is slightly different from what Jane Dudley and the other teachers are teaching in the school. I'm sure Miss Graham doesn't want us or anyone else to be a copy of her school as it was or is, but to be ourselves, and this we have become in the last few years, and it's requiring a certain amount of adaptation.'[3] Always at pains to insist that he was creating a British style, Cohan's class work and choreography softened the Graham-style angularity and accentuated the flow inherent in Graham's movement vocabulary. Speaking to Margaret Dunn in 1976, he explained that his Graham-based style had 'changed considerably over the years since it needed to fit the requirements of the Company'.[4]

But how to become even more 'ourselves' and what sort of further adaptation was required? According to Peter Connell questions had been raised amongst the staff for a considerable time about the emphasis on American codified teaching such as Graham-influenced techniques: 'it was being recognised it didn't suit all-comers. It just wasn't right for many of the students.'[5] The influence of a new generation of students on the School was also a factor in challenging the Graham ethos. One of these was the now established choreographer, Kim Brandstrup. Brandstrup arrived as a mature student at LCDS in 1980 from a film studies background in Denmark. 'In Denmark, [I was surrounded by] an environment of music, painting and film, and when at school there was an hour every morning when, totally unstructured, we moved to music. So movement was lodged in my body even when I started. I was studying film but I had this physical urge to dance as well, so I thought if I don't do this now it will be too late and I can always make movies. But of course me coming from the outside, I wanted Merce Cunningham and Pina Bausch – those were the real heroes of the younger generation. So I was always in a rebelling mood, a questioning mood, whatever I was given.'[6]

For other students, like the dancer Sean Feldman, at LCDS from 1983 to 1986, the Graham-based approach was still powerful, and it was Dudley who made the greatest impression: 'probably the most significant influence on me from that time was the passion Jane put into her teaching and into us as students. She was very demanding at times; but she always encouraged such a sense of beauty and elegance in the movement that it lifted you up somehow. If I think of some of the dancers who were at the school then, they were clearly inspired to move in a way that took them beyond technique and beyond themselves in every way.'[7]

Another former member of the Graham Company who had rethought and re-shaped her Graham heritage was Juliet Fisher.[8] She taught at the School from 1972 to 1999, developing her 'unique and distinct methodology for movement'.[9] Among her followers were the choreographer Jonathan Lunn and the dancer Lauren Potter: 'exercises accumulated in terms of length and complexity, rigour and stamina – everything built. They created an intriguing sensibility and sensitivity in the body as you tried to fathom out what she was playing with … You had to excavate into your own body to get a glimmer of what she was after. It could be frustrating, but once you unlocked the code in your body it made perfect sense and came alive.'[10]

Although Dudley was grounded in Graham, she recognised talented teachers who came from different backgrounds. She fought to attract the ex-Cunningham dancer and teacher Viola Farber on to the staff, [11] as someone who had strong ideas and was not afraid to voice them: 'it seems to me that there is a controversy going on at the LCDS that no longer exists anywhere else in the Western world: is Graham technique the only valid contemporary dance technique? In France there are numerous contemporary dance companies and independent dancers who have never done a contraction in their lives. In the United States it has not been considered necessary since the early 1950s to sit on the floor for a long time to learn to dance.'[12] Farber, who taught at LCDS from 1984 to 1986, complained about the difficulties she encountered which included 'teaching students to use their bodies in a different way from that to which they are accustomed. This includes lengthening and lifting the muscles rather than squeezing and clenching, using minimum rather than maximum force to achieve a move etc., moving with a basic simplicity, like a finely-toned human being, and not heroically, like a dancer – this latter being again a very limited and stereotyped idea of what [moving like a dancer] must be.'[13] Farber made a strong plea 'to recognize that not everyone is suited mentally, spiritually, emotionally, or physically to just one kind of anything'.[14] According to Connell, changes in technical training were afoot, although there was no specific time at which 'everyone sat down and said the days of formal Graham technique are over, but it just evolved that way'.[15]

Outside LCDS, in the wider cultural world of British contemporary dance, new and different influences were being recognised, adding to the questions being raised at the School about its technical training. In 1973 the influential Dartington College of Arts appointed the American dancer Mary Fulkerson as Head of Dance, and she introduced the form of technical training 'broadly known as Release'.[16] Fulkerson's Anatomical Release Technique preceded the introduction of the term 'somatics' by the philosopher/teacher, Thomas Hanna, in 1977, although Release and somatics share philosophical and practical principles. Teaching processes that come under the umbrella of somatics follow a more student-centred policy according to which the dancer is no longer focussed on replicating existing models of dance technique and performance. Rather they are encouraged to abandon the tension associated with striving towards prescribed goals. This philosophy of letting-go opens up new channels of achievement in accordance with the potential of the individual, an approach to teaching which became increasingly influential in contemporary dance studios.

From 1978 onwards the Dartington Festivals spread Fulkerson's ideas,[17] and by this time other American radicals had joined Fulkerson, such as Steve Paxton who introduced Contact Improvisation. They offered a less authoritarian form of teaching based on 'suggestion, invitation, improvisation, and collaboration',[18] and were key figures in producing a platform for alternative and fresh approaches to technical training and choreography throughout the 1980s.[19] Alston and other members of Strider had visited Dartington as early as 1973 and experienced Fulkerson's work,[20] but the first mention of classes in Release or Contact Improvisation at LCDS was not until the 1990s. Up until that time, the School concentrated on technical training directed towards the repertory performed by LCDT, still predominantly characterised by Cohan's Graham-influenced choreography.

As an alternative to the rigorous technical training during the 1970s and 1980s the School did not ignore the inner life of the students under its care. Foremost among those opening up other avenues of self-knowledge was Gerda 'Pytt' Geddes, who taught Tai Chi at the School from 1970-

1996. Pernille Charrington experienced a rare depth in her classes: 'she gave the most amazing qualities to really feed your soul and your centre so that you could find out who you are and ground you'.[21] Tharp also was fascinated by references to yoga principles in classes given by Bill Louther: 'when he talked about Kundalini, a yoga practice that influenced Graham, you wanted to know what he was talking about. Then in the Tai Chi class, when I was describing the physical sensation I was having to Pytt Geddes, she said "that's the opening of your third eye" – well, when people talk about things I have never heard about, I become very curious and I wanted to make the connection between the technique I learnt from teachers, Kundalini yoga and Tai Chi.' Geddes's work continued through those such as her former student Khin Titsa and the dancer Tim Lamford, who spread 'her particularly gentle way of teaching and educating, of grounding and centering, of breathing the dance and the power of living, and of the subtle energies that are involved, in dance, in Tai Chi, in art and music'.[22]

The Tai Chi classes unified the mind, body and spirit, and in the mid-1980s students could get further spiritual resource from the top man himself, Robin Howard. He ran a class called 'the dancer in context' or 'Robin's Course', as it was familiarly called. In the early 1980s Howard had undertaken a three-year part-time course at the Institute of Psychosynthesis, and he was convinced that this journey into self-knowledge and self-development would complement the dance-centred training in the School. Aided by two visiting practitioners, and with the occasional support of Cohan, Davies and Fonaroff, these were sessions that took place on Friday afternoons in his flat on Sandwich Street.[23] The dancer Sean Feldman was one of those who took part: '[Robin] was interested in the student's personal development and he took time to talk to us about our thoughts, feelings and general well-being. Our time together as a group was not really structured. He would just encourage us to be open about expressing ourselves in whatever way we felt we needed to or was appropriate to us individually and as a group. I think Robin was mainly concerned that the course offered us as much support for our personal development as people, not just dancers, as possible. He felt that was important and this was one way of providing that.'[24]

The emphasis on the deeper qualities offered by those closely connected with Graham was evident in how Cohan and Dudley worked with the dancers, as Ross McKim remembers: 'I never heard Cohan actually use the word "spiritual". He appeared concerned – in class, rehearsal and the activities that surround these – with "inner" transformation. At least some of us in the company understood he meant that this must take place in us, largely through studio work, before it could be evident in performance.'[25]

McKim felt there was a quality produced through Cohan's and Dudley's teaching 'which was not just Graham' technique but 'the almost religious enthusiasm they transferred' through it. This was a view shared by Sean Feldman who experienced a similar atmosphere in the School: 'some of the dancers who were at the school then were clearly inspired to move in a way that took them beyond technique and beyond themselves in every way'.[26] The students' near-religious experiences at LCDS continued even into the early 1990s. The choreographer Arthur Pita who undertook an MA at LCDS in 1991 refers to his technical training as 'like being in a church', describing classes that were driven by 'passion and intelligence'.[27]

Nevertheless, for Tharp, as for many other students studying at LCDS in the early 1980s one of the most significant advantages was the daily proximity of LCDT and the opportunity to learn professional standards from watching the dancers at work: 'if you wanted to see how it was really done, you went to studio 8 and you pressed your nose against the window and just watched and learnt and got inspired, and that was one thing that made it very special in the school. Not to say that everyone aspired to join LCDT but I think that there were few people who weren't inspired by them even if that wasn't their goal.'[28] Isabel Tamen, Executive Director of Richard Alston Dance Company, who studied at LCDS from 1982 to 1985, echoes Tharp's enthusiasm for peeking through the window of studio 8: 'every day, whenever I had a break between classes I could see these amazing dancers with Bob Cohan teaching class. He was inspirational. I thought I would never be good enough but that was something to aim for.'[29] For Mary Evelyn, also a student at LCDS during this period it was the opportunity to watch individual company members practising in quiet moments: 'when you walked into one of the studios before class, one of the Company might be warming up or working through a series of movements and I found it inspirational to observe the precision and care they took and the depth of their investigation into movement.'[30]

The inspiration communicated to the dancers by the proximity of the Company fed into their own performance experience, which the School fostered in different ways. In addition to the ongoing end-of-term workshops and the annual graduation performances, in the spring of 1983 students took part in performances in Southwark Cathedral of José Limón's *Missa Brevis* (1958) and Cohan's *Stabat Mater* (1975). Spring and summer performances were scheduled for The Place theatre in June and July 1983 and included a 'special showing' of student choreography. In 1980 a fourth year of study was introduced to maximise the opportunity of gaining experience of being on stage, and in 1983 the fourth year 'Performing Unit' visited places such as Laban, the Royal Academy of Dancing and the University of Kent. The Performing Unit led to the formation of 4D in 1989 as a postgraduate touring company providing a bridge between dance training and a professional career. 4D was re-launched as EDge in 2002 and in 2018 became known as EDGE.

Clearly Contemporary Dance Trust had much to be proud of and at a gala performance of LCDT in aid of the student scholarship fund at Sadler's Wells in 1984, Robin Howard complimented 'not only the growth of the Company and the School, but its worldwide reputation, supplying dancers for LCDT but also for Paul Taylor, Twyla Tharp and Martha Graham'. However, the financial situation continued to be precarious with Howard appealing for a 'lot more money' in order to ensure the maintenance of such excellent artistic standards.[31] Although the School could now offer prospective students a BA degree qualification, the relentless cuts to Council budgets all over the UK meant that students with limited means would struggle to receive discretionary grants. In 1980 Jack Norton, the CDT's long-standing financial director, put his finger on the funding pulse when he wrote that: '[LCDS] would have few financial problems if it shared the benefits of capital support and mandatory granting ... Its continuing progress and the promising careers of the many brilliant young dancers are threatened by a phase of unprecedented financial restraint.'[32]

This climate of restraint and cutbacks focussed a large part of Richard Ralph's energy into persuading the hard-pressed Councils to support talented students, and this was followed up by his drive to establish a scholarship fund in the early 1980s. This was and continues to be generously funded by the Leverhulme Trust, helping students on BA and MA courses. At the same time Ralph also saw the benefits of promoting the School on an international level, offering prospective students overseas the chance to audition, first in Denmark, and then expanding to Spain, Norway, Sweden, Switzerland, Australia, New Zealand, and to South East Asia – South Korea, Taiwan and Singapore: 'this helped to keep the school solvent without diluting standards, and we thought the internationalisation of the school added much to it'.[33] Ralph's international drive also extended to the United States, forging alliances and student exchanges, many of which still exist, with the Juilliard School and the State University at Purchase both in New York, the California Institute of the Arts and also the Universities of Hawaii and Utah, and Cornish in Seattle.

But the financial equilibrium of CDT became further unbalanced as the 1980s progressed, and the effort to maintain the reputation of LCDT as a major force within the contemporary movement became an additional financial burden.[34] From the mid-1980s onwards the erstwhile highly regarded LCDT aesthetic began to lose its currency. British choreographers such as Lea Anderson and Lloyd Newson were beginning to find their individual voices, with Lloyd Newson (who completed a one year course in choreography and dance at the School in 1980-1981) forming his physical theatre company DV8 in 1985. DV8 was one of the early companies commissioned by John Ashford, appointed Theatre Director of The Place in 1986. Throughout his 23 years at The Place he sought and presented challenging dance companies, and at the end of the 1980s created *Resolution*, The Place's annual festival of new choreography. A new era of independent dance had begun to flourish and multiply, and British audiences were becoming increasingly exposed to ideas arriving from America and Europe through the activities of Dance Umbrella, whose wide-ranging events had introduced international companies since it began in 1978. That was also the year that Pina Bausch's Tanztheater Wuppertal, with productions marked by interdisciplinary styles of movement, speech and cabaret, made its first visit to the UK at the Edinburgh Festival, with her debut in London in 1982.

While contemporary dance in Britain may have been thriving, this burgeoning of new approaches and influences destabilised the hitherto dominant position of LCDT and CDT. In 1985, a year after Howard's praise for the School and Company, he wrote a letter to the *Financial Times* articulating the artistic and financial quandary he felt: 'we have, in a sense, already attained the status of an establishment organisation, but we exist to bridge a gap between the establishment and a public which does not fit into that category. We are risk-takers. If we play safe we are untrue to ourselves. We now do not have sufficient funds to venture into the unknown, which is what we should do and have done so well in the past. A short-term solution to our problem is to play safe. If we do so, we shall die. And deserve to die, because people will eventually become bored.'[35]

This public airing of the Trust's problems unsettled the CDT board, and the view of the Arts Council towards both Howard and CDT. By January 1988 Howard had become aware of an 'undercurrent of the Board turning against him in his role as Chairman',[36] and by September this feeling had grown to the extent that Howard placed on the agenda for the September Board, 'The matter of the Chairman of the Board.'[37] The outcome of the ensuing discussion at which Howard himself was not present and no employees of the Trust including Cohan and Eager were allowed to vote,[38] was that Howard was sacked from his role as Chairman of the organisation which he had founded and which he had lovingly tended for three decades. Eager points out that members of the CDT Board increasingly included those from the corporate sector, 'people who might help us raise money or marketing people'[39] but who did not respond well to the more abstract spirit of love and togetherness that Howard constantly advocated. Howard was duly accorded the title Life President but according to Eager, this insensitive ousting destroyed him.[40]

Howard continued to be involved in dance following his appointment as President of the International Dance Committee of the International Theatre Institute, and embarked on a project to interview major choreographers with a view to developing a new form of dance training,[41] but this project was disastrously cut short when he had a series of strokes, and he died on 12 June 1989, at the age of 65. Cohan[42] had already announced his retirement from the helm of LCDT (though he remained on the board of CDT), and it fell to Richard Ralph and the teaching talent at the School to steer the LCDS into the 1990s without the two founding fathers of the whole enterprise. This would be a decade of dramatic change and renewal, when students lost their route into the Company, and Ralph would need to find replacements for two of the longest serving members of his faculty – Jane Dudley and Nina Fonaroff.

1   Interview with Howard, 1974, for Oral history Project, Dance Collection, New York Public Library

2   Ibid.

3   Ibid.

4   Cohan in interview with Margaret Dunn (1976). *Yorkshire Arts Association.* Contemporary Dance Trust Archive, V&A Museum

5   Interview with Connell, September 2015

6   Brandstrup in Private Passions, 1 November 2015 BBC R3

7   In McKim (undated) p.55

8   Fisher was a guest artist with LCDT and with Second Stride, as well as working with many choreographers from Merce Cunningham to Siobhan Davies. As Benjamin Ord said: 'Fisher trained many students in different countries who are now in 'positions of prominence around the world' quoted in Ralph 2015, p. 99.

9   Benjamin Ord quoted by Ralph, *Dancing Times* October 2015, p.99

10 Lauren Potter and Jonathan Lunn quoted by Ralph Ibid

11 Email communication with Richard Ralph, 26 November 2018

12 Letter from Farber to Howard (undated), Contemporary Dance Trust Archive, V&A Museum

13 In Slayton 2006, pp.227-228

14 Ibid. p.229

15 Interview with Connell, September 2015

16 Nicholas 2007, p.190

17 Ibid.

18 Hennessy (undated)

19 Ibid.

20 Nicholas 2007, p.188

21 Interview with Charrington, January 2016

22 Young 2013, p.6.

23 Interview with Eager, March 2019

24 Feldman in McKim 2004, p.58

25 McKim in McKim 2004, pp.5, 7

26 McKim and Feldman in McKim 2004, p.53

27 Pita in Jennings 2015

28 Interview with Tharp, July 2015

29 Interview with Tamen, July 2015

30 Informal conversation 2016

31 Clarke and Crisp 1989, p.173

32 Norton in Clarke and Crisp, p.138

33 Email communication from Ralph, 26 November 2018

34 Clarke and Crisp 1989, p.173

35 Howard in Pritchard 2010

36 Jackson 2013, p.279

37 Jackson 2013, p.279

38 Ibid.

39 Eager in McKim 2004, pp.95-96

40 See Jackson 2013, pp.278-279

41 Jackson 2013, p.283

42 Robert Cohan was awarded a knighthood in the Queen's Birthday Honours of June 2019 for 'Services to Choreography and Dance'.

Chapter 9

A new focus for The School: The Company closes – the 1990s

In 1991 LCDS was urgently looking for a replacement for Jane Dudley, who with her profound Graham knowledge had dominated the School as Director of Dance Studies for 21 years. The organisation identified a possible successor after a widespread search and interview process. This was someone who was strongly connected to Graham and had danced in her company, but who had then formed a close connection with the work of Paul Taylor for over ten years. The chosen candidate was Susan McGuire, who received a phone call from Ralph just at a time when she was looking for a new direction. She joined the School as Head of Contemporary Dance in 1991 and found herself facing an immediate challenge: 'the first couple of years were really tough. There was quite a bit of resistance to the fact that I was American and many people now thought a Brit should be coming into that post – which I understood completely. There was a very Graham-based ethos when I got there. I helped shift that a bit.'[1] McGuire, who was an outstanding rehearsal director, stated that 'having had Paul's work in my body for so long, I hope I was able to bring all of that to the students'. She was able to teach them 'big chunks' of Taylor's rep including parts of *Airs, Esplanade, Junction,* and his *Musical Offering* of 1986 to music by Bach, which for McGuire was Taylor's masterpiece: 'it is so profound and so primitive, it's not lyrical [or] balletic'.[2]

One student who greatly valued McGuire's approach and her extensive career as a performer was Martin Lawrance, who went on to dance with the Richard Alston Dance Company, before becoming its rehearsal director and a freelance choreographer. He said that he 'could never have asked for a more amazing teacher. She really guided us in our three years there, she was fantastic and I learnt so much. She used to dance for Paul Taylor, and so it was a softer form of Graham. I remember, I think it was in my second term of my first year, she said, "Martin you've got everything, you're very organised now just *d a n c e* – you know, just actually move." You could go up to her and chat and she would ask you how things were going and you could tell her that you were struggling in this or that. It was a real conversation that she seemed to have with all the students. She was like your big sister or your mum and if you come down to a school in London like LCDS, it's hard work and you expect it to be hard work, but to have this person who actually talks to you and guides you, it's amazing.'[3]

Robin Howard surely would have approved of McGuire's student-friendly approach and her ability to create a family atmosphere at the school. She was analytical, yet realistic, in the way that she worked to a 'five-year plan' which 'really took six'.[4] During her eight years at LCDS, McGuire 'designed a curriculum', taught classes and repertory and was able to 'hire in all the choreographers for 4D, the LCDS postgraduate performance company'.[5] It is clear from fellow-teacher Connell that McGuire introduced a more stable note in the constantly searching question of what technical training to offer the LCDS students: 'the teachers that came in and the diversity of the work that was being done in the country gradually altered the emphasis on Graham although there was a lively debate about such matters. When Susan came, that settled down a bit because her background was Paul Taylor, though she also understood and knew Graham. So she was good for the School, although we also had difficult personalities amongst the faculty who were resistant to change.'[6]

The School was further strengthened when the American choreographer Victoria Marks was appointed Head of Choreography after Nina Fonaroff's retirement. Marks took up her post in January 1992, but had already worked as a visiting teacher to the School on a Fulbright Fellowship in 1988, when she had created her compelling work for four female dancers *Dancing to Music*. Celebrated for her 'post-Judson minimalism and enthusiasm for working with non-professional dancers',[7] Marks brought a conceptual approach to her choreographic teaching, encouraging the students to abandon the strictures of technical training in order to explore their individual creative drive. Whilst students were increasingly advised to 'leave steps outside the door when going into choreography',[8] Marks appears to have followed Fonaroff, at least in spirit, since, according to Brandstrup, whilst 'she was incredibly analytical', she was in no way 'prescriptive – she was always respectful to who I was as an individual, letting me find my own way'.[9]

During Marks' relatively short tenure as Head of Choreography (1992-1995) more emphasis was given at the School to newer forms of contemporary dance practice. As mentioned in the previous chapter the School was slow to respond to Mary Fulkerson's Release style of teaching, even though Alston was introduced to it in 1973. There's a reference to Steve Paxton teaching some classes of Contact Improvisation in the 1980s,[10] and through her choreographic classes in the 1990s, Marks claims she introduced Release, as well as some sessions of Contact Improvisation.[11] The choreography department was bolstered in September 1992 when Karen Greenhough joined Marks, bringing with her a wealth of experience as a dancer and choreographer in her native

Canada and being awarded the prestigious Bonnie Bird Prize for New Choreography in 1992. She would be a mainstay of the undergraduate faculty for nearly twenty years, leaving in September 2013, and, like Marks, encouraged the students' exploration of conceptual movement. She also reinforced a sense of professionalism and theatricality in the way that she organised and oversaw presentations of student choreography for informal 'sharings' and for more public occasions such as showcases in the theatre. Among the choreographers who blossomed under her approach were such talents as the independent choreographers Eva Recacha and Frauke Requardt.

In the early 1990s, then, the School maintained a balance between the newer ideas circulating in the wider dance community as expressed by Marks and Greenhough, and traditional contemporary dance training represented, for example, by McGuire and by Juliet Fisher. Hilary Stainsby, who would later join the faculty, arrived at the School in 1995, and it was Fisher who she particularly remembers: 'there was already a recognition that things were shifting and moving on. There was a new generation of teachers, teaching more hybrid techniques. When I was there my main teacher for the three years was Juliet Fisher. Even though there was a real sense of departure in her work it was still very much rooted in Graham-based floorwork. I particularly followed the connectivity that she used, and things like the level of muscularity and resistance to the space. She used resistance to create a real sense of musculature and work in the body that didn't come across in other techniques, but when I was in other techniques I really appreciated their lightness and freedom, as her work was really quite heavy and dense, although the strength that it gave you was extraordinary.'[12]

From Stainsby one can get an idea of what was available in other specialist contemporary dance establishments in the mid-1990s. Before she made her choice, she had visited the Northern School of Contemporary Dance, Trinity Laban and LCDS, ruling out Rambert because of her lack of ballet training: 'I preferred the environment at LCDS and what appeared to be a really invigorating group of students, all striving towards the same thing. I also can remember seeing all the postgraduate companies perform – there was Verve, or maybe it was just the Third Years from Northern, there were Transitions from Trinity Laban and 4D from LCDS. At that point it was dancers who had done the BA at those institutions that were in 4D, and I felt that the standard of 4D was stronger than the others. I thought that LCDS trained the best dancers.'[13]

In September 1991, Martin Lawrance had taken a slightly different route to LCDS. It was the 1989 visit made by LCDT to the Warwick Arts Centre that captivated him: 'wow, I really enjoyed that. They did Dan

Wagoner's *White Heat* and it had Aletta Collins, Isabel Tamen, Isabel Mortimer, Paul Liburd – nowadays I look up to these people, I'm friends with them, but that's what really got me interested in dance. When I first came to the school I wanted to join LCDT.'[14]

Lawrance certainly did not have his eye on an academic qualification. Unlike other students he had a limited background in dance: 'I was doing a BTEC in Performing Arts two years before I came to The Place. The first year I specialised in drama, and then my teacher said that I wasn't very good at drama, but the dance teachers thought I was good at the movement classes and I did a crash course in a kind of Límon and Cunningham. I had no money and Vivienne Freakley, the Head of Dance at Coventry Centre for Performing Arts, paid for my LCDS audition fees. I was accepted and so it was in the space of eight months when I started to dance and got a place here.'

Lawrance's journey reflects the School's openness to dancers with potential but little training: 'I didn't really know anything. My third ballet lesson ever was at the audition. We had a 45-minute ballet class with Ronnie Emblen and then a 45-minute contemporary class with Juliet Fisher. Ronnie put me in between two girls who knew what they were doing. I thought *frappé* was a coffee not a ballet exercise.' But despite being thrown in at the deep end, Lawrance was enraptured: 'I came from a little village in Leicestershire and it was amazing to move down to London. Everyone was smoking everywhere. In all the corridors and on the stairs you had to stand in fag butts – but it was so exciting.'

At this time in the history of LCDS, students were streamed according to training and ability, so the less experienced Martin Lawrance started in the bottom stream: 'we were streamed A, B or C and I was an A (the most elementary) for ballet and contemporary. Most of my friends who are still dancing were A or B, but the Cs have long gone. Their standard was much higher whereas we didn't really know what we were doing, but we are the ones who are still working now, for example the choreographer Hannah Gilgren. The second year was divided into Ds and E. I got advanced to E in my second year and I stayed there for the third year and I had Juliet Fisher for another term. You had to be very flexible in the hips. Splits was about the 4th exercise in the class and at 8.45 in the morning my body wouldn't do that. Juliet struggled with me until my third year – she used to fail me in almost every contemporary assessment, but then in my third year she gave me As and Bs, so perhaps there was a change in my attitude!'[15]

Lawrance began on the BA ordinary degree that had just replaced the 3-year Certificate course, and he achieved sufficiently high grades to transfer in his second year to the BA Hons.[16] Although his main ambition was to dance and choreograph, the School, as it did with other students, carefully led him into what was for him the daunting world of academe: 'I used to enjoy my time in the studio choreographing, but writing essays just wasn't for me. I don't know how, but I got a 2.2, which I was really proud of because I thought I would get a 3rd or a fail. When it got to my dissertation, I wrote about what was on offer for deaf people within the deaf community, whether higher education, youth groups or whatever (my parents both being deaf). I just scraped by on that dissertation but in the third year the grades for my technique bumped me all the way up. All of a sudden they saw something in me and I was getting distinctions in my rep. Our third year rep project was *Rainbow Bandit* by Richard Alston. We had a project for six weeks when Linda Gibbs came in and taught us the work – we had two casts and performed it in the theatre and we were assessed on that performance.'[17]

That vivid appreciation of his time as a student shows that despite the death of Robin Howard, and a changing of the older guard at the School, Richard Ralph was ushering in a new age. But as part of CDT, the School was closely connected with the other activities of The Place, notably the Company, so it was a shattering moment for everyone when the Company was faced with the loss of its Arts Council grant and announced it would close after a farewell tour ending at Sadler's Wells on 18 June 1994.[18] The closure of the Company came like a thunderbolt, and as Judyth Knight reports, 'people could not believe what they were told'.[19] The entire School was gathered together in studio 8 one morning in December 1993 and informed that LCDT was to be wound up.

In a climate of diminishing enthusiasm for mainstream contemporary dance and a mounting interest in small and middle-scale companies offering a 'new wave' of multidisciplinary works, the Arts Council was not prepared to continue funding both LCDT and Rambert. Following acrimonious wrangling with the Arts Council, the Board of Contemporary Dance Trust under the Chairmanship of Laurence Isaacson, was forced to close LCDT.[20] Connell recognised the immediate effect the closure would have on the School: 'this Company, which had set the benchmark for technical and performance excellence in the School since 1967, and had provided the goal to which so many aspiring students joined LCDS and pursued their course of training, was gone'.[21]

For Lawrance who had peeked through the studio windows at the Company dancers for the first half of his three year course, the future had suddenly changed: 'the Company were rehearsing in studio 8 and we would come up and watch all the time. When it got to the second term of the 3rd year, two 3rd years each day would go and take company class, but suddenly we were told the Company was folding. That was what we were aspiring towards, so there were lots of tears, because we were hoping to get into the Company. Just after that I auditioned for 4D, and I was very happy to get in. That's when I got to know Richard Alston's work properly. We did one of his pieces, and during that year he offered me a job, so that's how I got to work with him.'[22]

The disbanding of London Contemporary Dance Theatre signalled the end of an era for Contemporary Dance Trust, and faced with a continually changing dance environment a decision on a replacement for LCDT had to be made with some urgency. John Ashford, as Theatre Director of The Place, continued to ensure that new work at the adventurous end of the contemporary dance spectrum was well represented. During his 23 years at The Place (he stepped down in 2009) 'the theatre established itself as the unrivalled proving ground for a new generation of independent contemporary choreographers from Britain and around the world'.[23] As well as supporting the pioneering companies of the 1980s, such as DV8, Matthew Bourne's New Adventures (then Adventures in Motion Pictures) and Wayne McGregor's Random Dance, he inaugurated both the *Resolution* festival of new choreography, the *Spring Loaded* season, and in 2004 gained sponsorship for The Place Prize, the most valuable prize for contemporary dance choreographers, awarded biennially until 2013. Ashford also presented the first UK performances of international artists such as Wim Vandekeybus, Sasha Waltz and Rui Horta.

However, CDT in discussion with the Arts Council was still committed to having a resident company at The Place. On the short list was a variety of groups and companies, but it was decided that Richard Alston was the clear choice, as someone who had had experience of being an Artistic Director (during his time at Rambert), but who also had long connections with LCDS as one of its first students and as a choreographer for LCDT. Alston was therefore invited to become overall Artistic Director of The Place and to form a new smaller-scale dance company to be resident in the building, and so in 1994 the Richard Alston Dance Company was born.

When LCDT closed, CDT's Chief Executive, Peter Sarah, who had been in the post since 1990, left, necessitating further changes. Graham Marchant, who had been Director of Arts Coordination at the Arts Council, joined CDT as General Manager in October 1995, and together with Ralph, Ashford, and Alston, ran the organisation. For Ralph this was a time when everyone needed to pull together: 'it was a cooperative, with all of us on equal terms; Graham chaired meetings and was *primus inter pares*.'[24] One initiative which Marchant supported was Ralph's view that arts schools providing higher education could benefit if they formed a group: 'it struck me that we were the obvious examples of world-famous institutions that weren't properly funded. The musical equivalents all were, and the arts equivalents all were, but the dance and drama weren't. The trouble is that

Governments work in large categories, and we were a small category, and we needed to consolidate.'[25] Ralph had established links with RADA over the years, and this was pursued by Marchant, though it had to wait until the next era of LCDS to reach its full flowering, as more changes were around the corner, including the departure of Ralph himself.

After 17 years as Principal, Ralph resigned in 1996 in order to take up a new post as Principal of Westminster College in Oxford. He had worked hard to keep the School at the forefront of technical and creative dance education: 'we trained the students to perform to the highest standards – we had to be at the cutting edge. If you fail to deliver that or to give that to students, they cannot survive in a profession that is constantly demanding.'[26] In this way he was confident that the School would maintain its place as a useful member of 'the dance ecology'.[27] Following Ralph's departure Marchant decided to add the position of Principal to his responsibilities of General Manager. This was a considerable task and it occurred at a particularly challenging time, as the old order of both School and Company gave way to the new.

1   Robertson (undated), retrieved February 2016

2   Ibid.

3   Interview with Lawrance, August 2015

4   Maguire in Robertson (undated), retrieved February 2016

5   Ibid.

6   Interview with Connell, September 2015

7   Morris and Nicholas 2018, p.113

8   Interview with Alston, August 2015

9   In Parry 2016

10   Email communication from Ralph, 23 October 2017

11   Email communication from Ralph citing Victoria Marks, 23 October 2017

12 Interview with Stainsby, July 2015

13 Ibid.

14 Interview with Lawrance, August 2015

15 Interview with Lawrance, August 2015

16 From 1991, LCDS students without A levels could undertake an ordinary degree course (Ralph 1995, p. 599)

17 Interview with Lawrance, August 2015

18 Levene, L. (1994), www.independent.co.uk 15 June

19 Interview with Knight, September 2015

20 See Jackson 2013, pp.295-298

21 Interview with Connell, September 2015

22 Interview with Lawrence, August 2015

23 Pritchard 2010

24 Email communication with Ralph, 14 January 2019

25 Ibid.

26 Interview with Ralph, June 2015

27 Ibid.

Chapter 10

Rebuilding, modernising, the creation of CDD – the end of the 1990s

To fill both leading roles, that of General Manager of Contemporary Dance Trust and Principal of LCDS, inevitably put considerable demands on Graham Marchant, particularly as he had begun the arduous task of raising funds for the modernisation and expansion of both the School and The Place. He had already raised considerable Lottery funding and appointed the architects Allies and Morrison, but he had insisted that he did not remain in any post for more than two years[1] and in mid-1998, after a relatively short time juggling the two posts, he returned to the Arts Council.

During this time the School was kept on the rails by Assistant Principal Peter Connell and Head of Contemporary Dance Studies Susan McGuire, although McGuire was to leave her post in 1998. Alston's role as overall Artistic Director gave him the opportunity to write a foreword to the 1996/1997 School prospectus which he began on a cautionary note: 'let's be honest about it, training to be a dancer is no easy task. Learning to control and articulate the body – reaching out to extend its range, digging deep to find the real root of its power – is an arduous process and there are no short cuts.' But he went on to underline that 'there are real rewards. Dance puts you directly in touch with your physical being: to become a dancer is to marry that physicality with clear analysis and understanding, and, all importantly, the well-springs of deep feeling.'[2]

Despite Alston's presence, Connell admitted he was highly relieved when 'we were putting in place the advertisement for a new principal.'[3] Not only had there been uncertainty over the leadership of the School, but the plan to radically improve The Place had become essential, both in terms of its role as a standard-bearer for contemporary dance and to upgrade its facilities and its general condition. Hilary Stainsby, then a third-year student earning some extra money working in the theatre bar, remembers unpleasant encounters: 'at the end of the night you had to take all the bottles for recycling. It would be dark, half-past ten at night. I used to get down to the café, just put my hand round the corner and switch the lights on, and not look. You'd hear tkktkkktkkk as all the cockroaches would scatter as soon as you put the lights on. The women's changing rooms were just full of them.'[4]

The departure of Marchant and McGuire created a critical vacuum, and the dancer and choreographer Sue MacLennan, who joined the faculty in 1995,[5] recalled Marchant proposing that the School should be led by 'an artist, a former dancer or choreographer'.[6] But the selection panel for the new Principal, which included MacLennan, decided that of the three candidates who were short-listed, the strongest to emerge from the interview process was not a dancer-choreographer, but a regional dance leader, Veronica Lewis. At the time Lewis was Director of Cheshire Dance Workshop and Advisory Dance Teacher for Cheshire County Council, but, as she says, the close connections she had maintained with The Place through her career stood her in good stead: 'in Cheshire I was commissioning and programming work that was coming out of The Place Theatre, not just from LCDT. I knew what was going on, practically, and also for some years I was on the Arts Council Dance Panel. I had also been involved with the first LCDT dance residencies up in Yorkshire, working with Margaret Dunn, and I had helped establish Rambert's education unit. I knew Richard Alston well and whenever the companies were up in Cheshire, they stayed at my house. Siobhan Davies', and Richard Alston's as well as Wayne McGregor's companies were up there, so I knew the scene very well.'[7]

Lewis's connections with contemporary dance went back even further, to her grammar school days in the early 1970s, though her practical dance exposure was based on a limited interpretation of Laban's methods: 'because of that, I didn't want to go to the Laban Centre, but I desperately wanted to go to LCDS to train. As a sixth former I used to skive off from school to come up to watch classes, to see performances, to do anything I could to find a way forward for dance. My background was in music, an art form that at school and in my family was taken seriously, whereas dance was not. I believed that there was a real gap in dance education, and the way in which dance had been portrayed. Many years later I learnt from Margaret Dunn[8] and she actually taught me about Laban, so that I realised that his work involved much more than flapping around being a sycamore tree as I had been taught at school by the hockey teacher.'[9]

'It was The Place that made an impact on me. I had a membership card for The Place Society which meant that I could come to performances and sit in those orange bucket seats and watch performances by companies like LCDT. I couldn't believe the fact that they didn't wear pointe shoes. I also watched classes taking place in the School through the windows. I wanted to train here but at that point ILEA wouldn't give grants for LCDS and I wasn't allowed even to audition as we couldn't afford it, which is why I trained at the Institute of Choreology because that was the only place that was free. But I grew up always wanting to dance and I suppose it was the things that happened to me early on that made me committed to change dance-in-education in the country, and I saw The Place as being a vehicle for that.'[10]

Lewis, therefore, was clearly on a mission when she applied for and then took up the post of LCDS Director (later Principal) in 1998: 'when I applied for the job local authorities no longer had the flexibility to be able to award grants, because the majority of the money had gone into schools themselves. I can understand the importance of doing that politically at the time, but it did mean dance training got pushed back again and it was quite a shock to discover that The Place physically was very run down.'[11] So Lewis immediately had to confront the urgent problem of student funding: 'my first day here, August 17, I remember sitting down and looking at the desk and thinking "what do I do now?" In came the financial director, David Burnie,[12] to introduce himself and immediately asked me what I was going to do about the following year's deficit. I remember thinking "oh no, not the sums already".'[13]

Finance was also at the top of Sue Hoyle's mind when she replaced Marchant as General Manager (later Executive Director) of CDT in 1998, since she assumed the management of the rebuilding, expansion and renewal of The Place and the School. Having worked with dance companies including London Festival Ballet (now English National Ballet) and Extemporary Dance Theatre, as well as her senior roles as Director of Dance for the Arts Council of Great Britain and then Deputy Secretary-General of the Arts Council of England, Hoyle was familiar both with the needs of dancers and students, and the complex planning and funding issues connected with a major project.[14] The Senior Executive Team on the project consisted of Hoyle, Alston, Ashford and Lewis, and Hoyle pays tribute to Burnie, who was 'responsible for finance and operations and absolutely critical throughout this period. I was responsible for fundraising as well as overseeing the capital project and the general direction of The Place.'[15]

The total cost was £7.5 million, over £5 million from the Lottery added to by a substantial contribution from the Kings Cross Partnership and the remainder from partnership funding. Work began in late 1999 and the most dramatic improvement was a completely new entrance to the School in Flaxman Terrace at the east end of the building, a triple-height, fully glazed elevation, providing valuable stretching zones for the dancers as they look down from the balconies into the reception area on the ground floor. As Kenneth Powell writing in *Architects' Journal* pointed out, this feature also 'allows passers-by to see the dancers exercising and is seen as a symbol of The Place's closeness to the community'.[16] For Hoyle 'this period was not just about improving the facilities of the building but also changing the business strategy and culture of the whole place, to make it more integrated and viable'.[17] A successful application was made to the Arts Council's strategy of Stabilisation and Recovery and that supported the 'programme of change' which included the implementation of a new, modern IT system and improved communication.'[18]

For Lewis 'there were three things we had to do very quickly. We needed desperately to sort the building out, to sort out the way in which The Place functioned in terms of the services that could be shared, and I was committed to sorting out some public funding for the School. Without mandatory funding, talented youngsters from low income families would miss out on opportunities in dance – the spread of male-female students, and the variety of socio-economic backgrounds would continue to be limited. So the following two years were a very steep learning curve.'[19] Nevertheless, this was a project for which Lewis was well qualified, as her work with Cheshire County Council and local authorities had brought extensive financial support to contemporary dance activities in the community and proved the benefit of 'trying to pull together disparate organisations but with the same vision. Suddenly I realised if we can do that in Cheshire surely we can do it here.'[20] She found a welcoming partner in HEFCE (the Higher Education Funding Council England), whose enthusiasm grew out of the Dance and Drama Awards which brought together students intending to join acting and dance professions. In 2000 HEFCE was to take a strategic position in support of the creation of a new Conservatoire for Dance and Drama,[21] and gave a green light to the discussions which were already under way.

Through her former experience Lewis realised it was counter-productive for specialist dance and drama schools to compete for a small pot of money, and she held a firm view that there should not be one funded dance conservatoire in England, but that 'any country needs a range of activities'.[22] In 1999, Lewis collaborated with John Myerscough 'who had set out the criteria for music conservatoires several years before in order to enable them to secure funding, and he then joined me here to try and sort out dance and drama'.[23] Lewis was able to build on the links with RADA that had begun with Ralph, and realised that RADA was 'our most powerful ally in this project and was just round the corner from The Place. Richard Attenborough (Chairman, then President of RADA 1973-2014) at that point was really keen to work with us, and the Labour Government was favourable. The then principal of RADA, Nick Barter, and John Myerscough and I sat round this table in my office trying to work out how to make something up that could be a collaborative model rather than a fighting against it model. HEFCE was really helpful, and the formation of the Conservatoire for Dance and Drama (CDD) started with RADA and us, and then it developed organically to include Rambert, Central School of Ballet, LAMDA, Northern School of Contemporary Dance, Bristol Old Vic and Circus Space.'[24] Following the creation of the CDD in 2001, the eight schools were eligible for the same levels of statutory funding as were the public universities. Students who attended CDD schools would therefore be entitled to student loans and pay fees in line with the current fee structure for universities. Lewis was appointed Joint-Principal of CDD from its inception until 2014, and therefore held three senior management positions – at the CDD, CDT and the School. In the years that followed she would rely on the full support of successive Assistant Directors, including Kirsty Alexander and David Steele.

While the negotiations for CDD were going on, the rebuilding project led by architects Allies and Morrison had got under way. This phase included the School, the Robin Howard Theatre and The Place entrance area and reception and would take two years, from 1999 to 2001. For Lewis this meant that 'we had to stop the post-graduate programme completely for a year, because there was no room for it, move the School to the west end of the building, and the Theatre and Artist Development initiative had to close. They began with the east end of the building, and then they did the theatre end.'[25]

Six new studios were created, as well as a lift providing disabled access, and more staff and changing room accommodation. Hoyle herself was concerned that the spirit of The Place had not changed and on the night of the opening she 'felt pretty nervous since Bob Cohan was going to be there. But Bob immediately told me "It's still the Place, Sue." His words made me realise that he had helped create an organisation with strong enduring qualities of quality, enterprise and love' that were embedded in the building and everyone who worked there.'[26] The Place and LCDS now had two imposing entrances at either end of the combined building, with a passageway below ground level linking both parts of the organisation, giving the students access to the improved restaurant, theatre and other amenities which completed this phase of the rebuild with a second phase adding two more studios planned for 2008.

The new millennium, then, began with the prospect of more secure funding for the students and the much-needed modernisation of the complete building. During this period much thought had been given to how the curriculum should be developed, since it was apparent that the future for students was changing rapidly. The School had to foresee what that future might look like, predicting what *Observer* dance critic Luke Jennings was to say a decade later: 'life for conservatoire graduates is desperately precarious. Most, given that the supply of contemporary dancers far outstrips demand, might find themselves performing, choreographing, producing, publicising, teaching, writing about dance or involved in dance therapy.'[27] LCDS was now engaged in preparing their students for that multi-faceted professional life, and the concept of training the 'dance artist' was firmly on the map.

1   Interview with MacLennan, April 2016

2   1996/7 Prospectus. Contemporary Dance Trust Archive, V&A Museum.

3   Interview with Connell, September 2015

4   Interview with Stainsby, July 2015

5   Sue MacLennan, Head of Choreographic Studies at LCDS, studied dance and drama at Dartington College of Arts and performed with the Rosemary Butcher Dance Company (1976-1988). As a choreographer she has collaborated with composers, visual artists and video/film makers and gained recognition for her improvisatory work, creating over fifty works, including a dance for EDGE (2006).

6   MacLennan 2016 reporting on Marchant's proposals

7   Interview with Lewis, October 2015

8   The 1976 Yorkshire residencies were sponsored by the Yorkshire, Humberside and Lincolnshire Arts Associations. Under the leadership of figures such as Sir Alec Clegg, Margaret Dunn and Jean Williams, enthusiasm for dance flourished in the West Riding of Yorkshire. There was encouragement for energetic and enthusiastic students such as Veronica Lewis and Gill Clarke to run classes and workshops and to prepare the ground for London Contemporary Dance Theatre's residencies. Clegg, Dunn and Williams were involved in the Yorkshire Movement Study Group at Woolley Hall.

9   Interview with Lewis, October 2015

10   Ibid.

11   Ibid.

12   David Burnie became Director of Administration and Finance early in 1990 having been Director of Administration Designate in the autumn of 1989. He retired in 2015 having made a consistent and significant contribution to the financial affairs of CDT. Emma Gladstone who presented Burnie with the Jane Attenborough Dance UK Industry

Award in 2011 called him 'a hidden gem who has been quietly and unassumingly helping to steer The Place through a myriad of major changes' www.onedanceuk.org

13   Interview with Lewis, October 2015

14   Sue Hoyle left her post as Executive Director of CDT in 2003, when she became Deputy Director of the Clore Leadership programme then Director in 2008. The role of general manager of The Place was filled by the freelance arts manager, Nigel Hinds in 2004. In 2007 Kenneth Olumuyiwa Tharp was appointed Chief Executive of The Place.

15   Email to the authors 2 March 2019. Hoyle also referred to the valuable work of the sub-committee consisting of CDT chair Ian Fisher, treasurer Graham Reddish, construction lawyer Ann Minogue and property developer Feargus Low.

16   Powell 2001

17   Email from Hoyle, 2 March 2019

18   Ibid.

19   Interview with Lewis, October 2015

20   Ibid.

21   Neelands, Lindsay, Freakley et al 2006

22   Interview with Lewis, October 2015

23   Ibid.

24   Interview with Lewis, October 2015. In March 2014 Circus Space was renamed the National Centre for Circus Arts. On 1 August 2019 RADA and LAMDA left the CDD.

25   Ibid.

26   Hoyle 2017

27   Jennings, July 2015

Chapter 11

Embracing the independent dance artist – the new millennium

When Veronica Lewis became Principal at LCDS, she wanted to broaden the scope of student expectation, developing shared responsibility between the students and the faculty: 'this meant that once we'd taken a student we were going to do the maximum to encourage and develop that potential – if we invest in a student we then have to work with them. Now that doesn't mean to say you're mollycoddling, as some may think. It means that you're very clear what you need from them and what they need from us, and unless there's that shared responsibility for your education you can't educate anyway. I think that what we've moved away from is an ecology of gurus, not saying "I did it this way, so you do it", but we're trying to show students *their* way in to doing things. We had to re-educate people not to expect that the only route into the profession was joining one of the big companies. We had to help them realise that there are many other opportunities.'[1]

Hilary Stainsby who joined the teaching faculty in 2009 accepted that planning for the future as a dancer had changed considerably from the time she was a student at the School from 1995-1998: 'in my day it was a case of needing to be the versatile person who could dance with Siobhan Davies or Wayne McGregor or whoever. Now the undergraduates are educated to create an environment where they can grow these little seeds of becoming dance artists. They might have some of that versatility but also have much more of a sense of who they are and who they want to be, where they locate themselves, and how they can generate work for themselves, without just waiting for the next audition.' Students, through the projects they undertake in their third year, 'are invited to think deeply about where their interests lie, what questions they have, where they place their work within a wider context, and then figure out how they facilitate something to come out of that process'.[2]

The idea of the independent dance artist had been circulating for some time especially through the dancer and teacher Gill Clarke. Although not directly connected to LCDS, Clarke's presence in and influence on dance education was widespread. Clarke died in 2011 at the age of 56 and in their obituary Rosemary Lee and Siobhan Davies wrote that 'her enquiries as a dance artist extended into her teaching, one fed the other.

She believed passionately that young dancers would gain from deepening their own experience of movement through practices such as experiential anatomy, Alexander Technique, Feldenkrais Technique and other somatic approaches in order to become questioning, intelligent dancers capable of expressive, integrated and engaged dancing. Additionally, Clarke sought to give students opportunities to work with a range of choreographers and practitioners whose approach was open, enquiring and ethical. The success of her approach is evident in the abundance of thoughtful, creative dance artists who emerged.'[3]

Kirsty Alexander, who joined LCDS as Assistant Director of the School in 2004, had performed with Gill Clarke, Rosemary Butcher and Gaby Agis and was Head of Undergraduate Studies at Trinity Laban before coming to LCDS. Alexander was aware that the School wanted to go in a new direction, but this was a message that initially was difficult to convey: 'LCDS operated as part of a publicly funded higher education system and therefore its responsibilities vis-à-vis how students are treated, how they are admitted in the first place, what kind of feedback they get, was all part of a different system from the historical one which had been a great source of pride for the School. We still had applicants coming whose teachers had told them all about the historical version, so there continued to be those kinds of expectations from applicants. It was difficult for the School to find, what, in this very different world, was its identity and to Veronica's credit I think she wanted to move forward into the present-day world.'[4]

The move away from the 'historical version' of the School with its Graham-Cohan heritage may have been slow to be recognised by those in the outside world, but Lewis's vision for a more responsive climate at the School was changing this perception with the support of her faculty. Alexander was 'keen to develop choice with people identifying what kind of artist they wanted to be'. If by the time a student reached the third year of the programme they decided that they aimed towards Alston's company, she ensured that 'in their third year they concentrated on that kind of technique and those kinds of reps in order to achieve the high technical standard required for that company. If they wanted to be Contact Improvisers they might need a different kind of morning class that was appropriate for them.'[5] During the five years that she worked as Assistant Director at LCDS Alexander strove to achieve a 'radical rebalancing of different kinds of outcomes for different kinds of students – rebalancing the weight of the third year final technique exam, recognising that students were going to have different strengths and directions without aiming for everybody to be a jack-of-all-trades.'[6]

As an LCDS student from 2001-2004, the dancer-choreographer Ben Duke had already taken advantage of the new focus of the School and was candid about what he saw as his own shortcomings: 'I really struggled with the technique classes but there were people who were always supportive and patient, and gave me extra time and help.' Duke particularly singled out the American teacher and choreographer Rick Nodine: 'he was teaching improvisation and that involved Contact Improvisation but it also involved an idea of improvisation as performance. The thing that I really loved about those classes is that we were all treated as artists rather than the slight hierarchy of the technique-based classes. It also just brought so many of the things together. I felt like we weren't talking that much about performance in technique classes, and yet in these classes it was pure performance. That's all we were dealing with. And it opened up a whole load of ideas for me, and I felt I was able to bring in the acting training that I'd done before, and the words, and that all of those things could find a place in this kind of format.'[7]

The teacher and choreographer Rick Nodine had arrived at LCDS at the same time, 2001, as Duke was beginning his three year course. He immediately filled a significant gap 'teaching six or seven Contact Improvisation classes a week. Sue MacLennan taught some Contact Improvisation within her choreography classes, but I was hired as they wanted someone specifically to teach CI.'[8] Nodine first encountered Contact Improvisation in Philadelphia, and when he moved to Europe and London, he studied further with Steve Paxton, Nancy Stark-Smith and the British teacher Kirstie Simpson. Nodine saw its beginnings as rooted in America of the 1960s and 1970s, a time which 'was to do with being egalitarian, feminist and non-hierarchical'. In Contact Improvisation dancers build skills of dancing in partnership with others, using their weight, balance, and touch to explore the experience of moving. For Nodine it is 'partner dance that doesn't have a leader, very definitely not a male leader, in the way that you do with most social dances. It subverts most of the physicalities of partnering that came before it, in the way that anyone can support anyone else, their gender is not in question. When I first arrived I was not sure that all that many students knew about CI but now in 2018, everyone has got some sense of what's going on – not so much about the skills of CI but more about being comfortable to improvise. I teach very specific skills and patterns and then I create spaces for improvising with those principles and patterns. In this latter half of the near 20 years that I have been here, (the students) are often confident improvisers from the start.'

Nodine also sees his classes as benefitting potential choreographers and performers such as Duke: 'one of the major things that improvisation is useful for is ownership, so there's the possibility to express what you're interested in, which is probably what you're good at and to work from that place of "I like this, I'm good at this, I understand this and I offer it as my expression today here in class". It's not surprising that this translates into them building an identity as a choreographer also because they're affirming what they *can* do rather than re-enforcing what they can't do and that's one of the ways that you understand who you are as a dance artist.'[9] The confidence this approach gave Duke led him to found his company Lost Dog with Raquel Meseguer in 2004, winning a number of awards for his work including the Place Prize for choreography in 2011. The company has widened its activities to include workshops, residencies and freelance choreography. Although Duke has often performed as a soloist or in duet, his company work *Goat* for Rambert in 2017 earned him a prestigious Olivier Award nomination.

Starting an enterprise while still an undergraduate at LCDS has also been proof of student initiative. Antonin Chediny, who graduated in 2015, co-founded The Sparse Collective while a student in 2014, and said at the time: 'we've already done a few performances, we have a website and business cards coming up – it's all very much in development'.[10] For those such as MacLennan, this atmosphere of enthusiasm, endeavour and creativity was life-enhancing and inspiring: 'a feeling that I have maintained throughout the years I have been here is one of privilege that I am in touch with young people when such a big thing happens to them, to be around young people and sharing interests with them through their transformation over the three years'.[11]

This wider emphasis on the student as a self-managing dance artist provoked a critical debate in 2015 when three choreographers – Lloyd Newson, Akram Khan and Hofesh Shechter – issued a statement about what they perceived was a decline in standards they witnessed when holding UK auditions.[12] They singled out LCDS, Trinity Laban and the Northern School of Contemporary Dance and complained that although they wanted to employ graduates from those conservatoires, they found that the students often lacked 'rigour, technique and performance skills',[13] and were 'forced to employ better trained dancers from overseas.'[14]

The then Vice Principal and Director of Studies, David Steele, conceded that he found this criticism 'painful', but concluded that it 'made us stronger in our views about what LCDS stood for. I firmly believe that we can say that we aim to nurture and enable rather than "produce" dancers to order.'[15] A vision statement resulted, asserting the ambition that LCDS had as its goal 'to become an international leader in dance education, driving discovery and developing the art form'.[16] From the interviews in this chapter, it is clear that many graduate students prefer to have their own agency, and although students can choose to audition and are accepted into established British and international companies, many do not. They want to plough their own artistic furrow, and in their independent way fulfil the School's mission 'to create innovative and inspiring learning programmes that develop dance artists to the highest standard, preparing them to lead and shape the art form'.[17]

Four LCDS graduates who were among the many who followed this vision and became self-managing artists included Jamila Johnson Small,[18] Eleanor Sikorski and Joseph Toonga, each of them presenting highly individual dance and choreography. In Johnson Small's case this found its expression in interrogating social and aesthetic assumptions. Sikorski, as well as co-founding the dance project Nora with Flora Wellesley Wesley, has pursued a portfolio career in dance, cabaret, film and music,[19] and Toonga founded Just Us Dance Theatre[20] which fuses hip-hop, physical theatre, contemporary dance and spoken word.

The changing emphasis towards the nurturing of independent dance artists was a development that Howard foresaw in the earliest days of the School and the Place. As he wrote in 1969: 'contemporary dance is an attitude towards dance, not a technique. It is concerned with using movement, especially the movement of the human body to communicate something to an audience, and usually about human beings. The vital training is of the self, the artist, and the technical training merely the making, as it were, of an instrument for the particular artist. Thus contemporary dance and its technique must always be developing and changing to suit different needs of communication.'[21]

1   Interview with Lewis, October 2015

2   Interview with Stainsby, July 2015

3   Lee and Davies 2011

4   Interview with Alexander, July 2016. Alexander, who left LCDS in 2010, later became Co-director of Independent Dance (2015-2017).

5   Ibid.

6   Ibid.

7   Interview with Duke, March 2018

8   Interview with Nodine, 6 November 2018

9   Ibid.

10   Interview LCDS students virtual open day 2015. Established in 2014 The Sparse Collective went on to perform 'improvisation and collaborative making'. See also Twitter @The_sparse_co

11   Interview with MacLennan, April 2016

12   Jennings, July 2015; Mackrell, April 2015

13   Newson in Jennings, July 2015

14   Jennings, July 2015

15   interview with Steele, September 2016

16   LCDS vision and mission statements, 2016

17   Ibid.

18   jamilajohnsonsmall.wordpress.com

19   eleanorsikorski.com

20   justusdancetheatre.org

21   In Adshead and Mansfield 1985, p.4

Chapter 12
Fifty years on – and counting

The energy of the teachers and students at the School in 1966 created waves in the dance world that continue to have a major impact. Two of the very first full-time students, Richard Alston, who celebrated fifty years as a choreographer in 2017,[1] and Siobhan Davies, a half-century since she was at LCDS with Alston, have both been fully engaged with dance over those fifty years. Alston continued to make work with his company and internationally. Siobhan Davies broadened her activities as choreographer and founder of her own companies (1981 and 1988), when she established the Siobhan Davies Studios in London in 2006, a centre to support independent artists, offer classes, and enable performance projects.

Many students who came to LCDS in the 1960s and 1970s forged successful and long-lasting careers that have been cited in this account – choreographers like Kate Flatt, Anthony van Laast, and Jacky Lansley. It was a natural progression for many to become teachers, Patrick Harding Irmer and Anca Frankenhaeuser, for instance, taking their knowledge and experience to Australia. Others started their own companies, notably Celeste Dandeker-Arnold, co-founder of the mixed-ability Candoco, or were involved in forming Strider, X6, and other collective dance groups that challenged established forms of contemporary dance. These alumni of the early years built on the impetus created by LCDT and the School, helped extend the diversity of contemporary dance, and changed the face of dance in the UK and further afield. Succeeding generations of LCDS students have continued to confront the dance culture, enabling it to pursue new directions, amongst them the choreographer Aletta Collins, a graduate of the late 1980s, whose award-winning work ranges from opera, dance and theatre to film and music videos; and Jonzi D, who graduated in the early 1990s, and launched the international hip hop theatre festival *Breakin' Convention* in 2004.

Since the founding of the School, each incoming Principal of LCDS has needed to find solutions to the shifting environment, posed not just by new ideas in dance, but by political, social, and technological change. They have had to introduce fresh approaches to training, managing the ambitions of students, while at the same time grappling with financial pressures, and dealing with the ageing fabric of the building. In 2017 the School once again faced a major test. The board of CDT began to look for a new Chief Executive to replace Kenneth Olumuyiwa Tharp who left in

November 2016, and in September 2017 Clare Connor was appointed. But Connor found that her task immediately became considerably more formidable, when Veronica Lewis, the School's Principal for 19 years, announced that she would retire in December 2017.

Recognising the need to build a unifying identity for both School and Theatre, Connor took the decision that she would initially combine the post of Chief Executive, the person at the helm of all the activities of The Place, with that of Interim Principal of the School: 'as challenging as it is, it is a fantastic opportunity. I am the accountable officer, and I'm also the Chief Exec, so no longer does anyone externally need to talk to two people. That means the conversations I'm having with people are very clear about the 100% not the 50% of the organisation they're interested in. From the Arts Council, the CDD and our HEFCE partners there is one conversation.'[2]

Connor's connection to the School goes deep. She became a student in 1988, benefitting from the long-serving Jane Dudley and Juliet Fisher as well as the younger teachers like Anca Frankenhaeuser and Mary Evelyn. 'I came in drinking it in. I absorbed it. I learned to learn here, and I learned to love learning.'[3] Connor left the school in 1991 just before taking her degree in order to perform with Phoenix Dance Theatre, but was allowed to continue her studies, graduating with First Class Honours. Of the many influences in her approach to dance she cites Janet Archer, also an LCDS graduate, founder of the dance company Nexus, and a former Director of Dance at the Arts Council: 'she was at Nexus at that point and I remember her doing a session, and she talked about subverting the idea that those who can dance, dance, and those who can't dance teach. She wanted to challenge that and I heard that loud and clear. That went back to my formative experience of really valuing the education, the teaching I'd been part of.'[4]

Connor's PGCE qualification was followed by a focus on teaching, and then learning 'how to manage projects within an education framework, how you can secure money for projects within education, and then how to get the money to make that work happen'. Armed with this experience she became director of Stratford Circus Arts Centre in 2005, followed in 2014 with her appointment as Director of Business Development at London's Southbank Centre, before accepting the top job at The Place: 'although I've been away from dance as a pure art form on its own, it feels like coming home, and it feels like all the experiences I have had are things I can bring to this organisation.'[5]

The relative straightforwardness of student ambition when Connor was at the School in 1988 was summed up by her memory of Robin Howard's introductory meeting with the new intake: 'I remember putting my hand up when he asked the question every year – "who wants to join the Company?"'[6] In 2017 graduating students were asked what *their* hopes were on leaving LCDS. The answers were an example of the broadening of contemporary dance culture within the last two decades. No longer were the options straightforward, and the students voiced their independence: 'I am looking forward to freelancing as a performer whilst developing my own creative projects in film and improvisation,' 'after graduating from LCDS I am switching gears and moving into the arts management and the cultural policy sector,' 'the immediate future holds a year in Leeds as a member of Northern School of Contemporary Dance's postgraduate company VERVE. After that… uncertainty, excitement, glitter, fun and, of course, saving the world,' 'I want to continue to make work, pursuing a choreographic/performance [career], as well as a part-time perfumer, and part-time chocolatier,' and for some the future was a leap into the unknown: 'I have no idea. That scares me and excites me (but lots of boogie for sure).'[7]

This sense of adventure and individual ambition is one that chimes with Siobhan Davies. Siobhan Davies Dance, particularly through its connection with partner organisation Independent Dance, enshrines as one of its aims 'to support, sustain and stimulate dance artists in their ongoing development as professionals'.[8] By 2018 Davies had noticed 'a present generation of artists younger than myself, whose work can investigate the political and social dimensions of dance and choreography. Their work has been honed by different circumstances and questions from when I began. During my beginnings we were trying to establish our art within a society and on a public which had limited experience of dance as a contemporary medium. I always hope that I can evolve and accompany the new thinking of artists making *now*. There's an intelligence there that I really like being part of, and if our organisation, our studios, can support part of that, that's what I want it to do. I believe dance-based artists want to be very relevant to now. I think of them as searching for what makes us different, as well as compatible to each other, to keep curious and expand our interests and connections. It's my hunger to look out for what artists are doing now, and to try with them to think ahead about what can happen.'[9]

Having experienced her early career as a dancer and choreographer in the Cohan-led London Contemporary Dance Theatre before setting off on her own, Davies recognised the courage and spirit of dancers determined to follow their own investigations and develop practices that make sense to them. 'Independence gives you huge financial problems, loneliness, and struggle, but it can hone something very particular and therefore make a distinctive contribution. It is exciting when instead of being a sole artist, a few can gather together and exchange what we know, and structure a work made by many. These situations give a sense of being in company for a chosen amount of time, rather than being permanently *in* a company, which can be repetitive and often leaves the artist without a distinct contribution. Each artist in these mixed circumstances needs to develop a portfolio of activities. Artists have always needed to be multi-faceted, they will do a huge amount to continuously sustain and evolve their practice. I notice that teaching in academia as well as achieving PhDs has increasingly become part of an artist's enquiries, alongside making and performing, and finding other ways to earn enough to maintain a life in the city.'[10]

The cliff edge facing graduates as they complete their training and emerge into the professional world has always been a nerve-wracking moment especially as students have far more choice than in the early decades of the School's existence. Contemporary dance has established itself on many different platforms – from the independent dancer described above by Siobhan Davies to the ambitions of young choreographers who want to follow in the footsteps of those who have established their own companies like Hofesh Shechter or Wayne McGregor. James Wilton, who graduated in 2009, launched his company in 2010, and has toured internationally, creating works for his dancers as well as other companies. Following closely behind was James Cousins, who formed his own company in 2014. Immediately after graduating in 2010, Cousins joined the cast for an international tour of Matthew Bourne's *Swan Lake*, and in 2011 he made a work for the *Resolution* festival, going on to win the inaugural New Adventures Choreographer Award. This culminated in a showcase of his own work at Sadler's Wells in September 2012: 'within two years of graduating I had a showcase at Sadler's Wells which was completely bizarre! Probably too fast in hindsight, but there was this momentum. It happened. It was like all my dreams had come true.'[11]

Although it was slightly delayed he then had his 'cliff edge' moment. 'I was so naïve and so young. I was 23. I was just making it up as I went along, and there was definitely a moment of fear. Over a year I had had this great mentoring from Matthew Bourne and been really supported. Any problem – just pick up the phone to Matt or email, and then there's the show at Sadler's Wells, and it's finished and you're like "whoooa... ok", freefalling from a huge height. There were a few years of manically trying to stick in the bricks to build the foundations and the first floor, and the second floor, and to sustain it.'[12] Together with Creative Producer Francesca Moseley, and building on his own independent choreographic commissions, Cousins' company soon established itself, with work in schools, youth groups, workshops and CAT schemes[13] providing financial stability for his company's touring schedule of performances. 'I'm in this amazing position that I can offer people work and the chance to create and to be an artist, and I really love being able to offer that. That makes all the hard work really worthwhile.'[14]

Preparing for this kind of enterprise Connor recognises is a vital part of the School's responsibility: 'we're looking at graduate destinations, and really understanding how that operates, and what it means for people. I think the idea of small business, and learning how to set up yourself is really important, whether you are applying for funding or part of a bidding process. In addition, obviously, to the technical training, we're supporting students to access and acquire that knowledge, and inside our organisation we have all that knowledge and experience.'[15]

The unique structure of CDT, with students and professionals involved in a buzzing hive of different activities throughout The Place and the School, is central to Connor's ambition to enrich the students' programme. In the first LCDS prospectus to be published under Connor's leadership, there is an emphasis on the breadth of what The Place offers – as a 'choreographic hub', home to a production house, a theatre, and being part of 'an inspiring and supportive artistic community' – with the School 'embedded' within it.[16] The intention of the three year BA course is that it supports 'the transition from student to professional practising dance artist'.[17] So the first two years have a broad mix of techniques – including Cunningham, Release, Contact Improvisation and Flying Low,[18] together with the study of choreography and choreology, the relationship of music and dance, critical thinking, and aspects of design – from costumes to lighting and video. With a solid basis of critical theory to draw from, the third years undertake the Negotiated Project (begun in the 2nd year), involving research into selected topics and presented in the form of a wholly-written dissertation of 6-8,000 words, or a practical choreographic performance, film, or costume-based project supported by a 3-4,000-word written component.

Throughout their time in the School, students work with established choreographers, often in specially commissioned works; they engage in collaborative work, and make their own dances, to be presented in the Robin Howard Dance Theatre and other venues. Unsurprisingly, when they look back on their three years, it is often the experience of performing that is their chosen highlight. For Conor Kerrigan in 2018 'the pinnacle moment at LCDS for me was performing *Overdrive* by Richard Alston at the Peggy Hawkins Gala Event', while Dorna Ashory picked out 'learning and performing *PassoMezzo*, choreographed by Ohad Naharin and taught by Chisato Ohno' as her 'proudest experience', and Elisabetta Pellegrini chose 'the Rafael Bonachela repertoire learned with Wayne Parsons'.[19]

The most ambitious event in recent years involved 45 LCDS students taking part in *Polaris*, conceived and choreographed by the Canadian choreographer Crystal Pite in 2014. Sixty-four dancers in total, drawn from LCDS, Central School of Ballet and Crystal Pite's own company performed this large-scale piece to critical acclaim at Sadler's Wells. Equally valuable is the performing opportunity offered by LC3, the undergraduate touring group formed in 2006, and an echo of the student X-Group in the 1970s, giving undergraduates the experience of touring to schools, colleges and small theatres. For postgraduates, who choose to complete a 4th year at LCDS, there is the chance to audition for EDGE, giving them a flavour of company life over a 10-month period, presenting new and existing works, leading to a PGDip (Postgraduate Diploma) or an MA. A similar qualification is open to 4th year students who audition and dance for professional companies both in the UK and abroad.

Over the three or four years a student is at the School, Connor aims to provide the means by which students can gain knowledge of all aspects of a professional life: 'that's artistic, commissioning, producing, touring, learning, participation and student experience, communications, development, fundraising, and operations for the whole site. Collaboration, and collaboration beyond dance, I think is central.'[20] She considers the Creative Industries Federation, formed in 2014 to be a powerful advocate for the arts in areas of politics, economics and society, as defining the new environment for arts organisations. As she says: 'the landscape has definitely shifted, and we have to understand the ecology in which we sit. It's important for the students to see the way in which we are located in a creative industries sector.'[21]

The mutual support encouraged by the Creative Industries Federation comes at a time when other changes have had a direct bearing on the landscape in which LCDS and the other members of the CDD are situated. In April 2018 the Government replaced the long-standing funding body HEFCE with the Office for Students. Alex Graham, LCDS Director of Student and Academic Services, described this new regulatory body as 'a hugely significant change in Higher Education – the biggest change ever – it far surpasses the 1972-1974 expansion in Higher Education'.[22] On behalf of its members, the CDD has completed successful registration with the Office for Students, stating that 'this means that our UK and EU students are eligible for government loans and grants in the same way as students from any other university'.[23]

Another major development is the option for schools and colleges to obtain their own Taught Degree Awarding Powers (TDAP). The model which the School pioneered, to have the Dance BA validated by an external university, has been superseded by this new self-validating authority.

With competition growing in the area of dance degrees – the *Which?* University guide for 2019 listed 54 UK universities where dance degrees of different specialisations were offered[24] – the acquisition of TDAP has become a desirable step and it is a strategic aim of the CDD to achieve this for its members. For Alex Graham the acquisition of TDAP 'would place us on a much firmer footing and allow us more opportunity to develop, if we choose to do so, new programmes. We could run very successful intensives here to an international audience. It's a changing climate and nobody is quite sure what that's going to look like, but if you stand on the side-lines and don't try to work within it you won't get anywhere.'[25] LCDS already offers a Virtual Prospectus, whereby potential students from across the globe have access to a comprehensive introduction to the teachers, classes and students available online through its website and social media platforms.

Certainly, the School's past record of attracting students from all over the world has been impressive. As well as students finding employment and opportunities within the UK, many graduates return to their countries of origin or aim at wider horizons. In 2018 that included the Theater St Gallen Dance Company in Switzerland, the Company Zappola in Italy, Staatsoper Bremerhaven in Germany, Arts Fission Dance Company in Singapore, and Szekesfehervase Dance Company in Hungary. And even further afield the MA graduate Xinxin Song returned to Beijing to make a work for the Young Artists Platform of Dance in China, with a performance at the National Centre for the Performing Arts.[26]

As the decades have passed areas of study and performance may have disappeared or developed in different ways, but the central core of technical skill sited within a contextual framework has been consistent throughout. The Graham/Cohan connection has given way to Cunningham and Contact; the study of dance history has been replaced by a more critical engagement with the conceptual aspect of dance; and alternative ways of gaining knowledge and awareness through the body have continued to be taught; for many years this was in the hands of the revered teacher of Tai Chi, Pytt Geddes, whose influence on students like Tharp or Charrington has been noted in an earlier chapter. In the new millennium Chisato Ohno introduced Gaga to the School, and joined the Faculty of LCDS in 2013.[27] Like Tai Chi, the Gaga practitioner searches for the deep sensations of the moving body in a technique evolved by Ohad Naharin in the 1990s. Whereas Tai Chi derives from an ancient Chinese martial art, Gaga's roots are in dance, and was developed by Naharin while directing and teaching the Batsheva Company in Israel from his conviction that 'physical pleasure from physical activity was part of being alive'.[28] Both practices, however, come within 'somatics' or a first person exploration of the lived and living body. Gaga sessions are entirely improvised – there are no exercises or set phrases of movement – rather the practitioner responds to imagery provided by the teacher, a means through which dancers realise their potential for achievement both within and outside the Gaga class.

A similar progression has also informed the performance part of the students' experience. The restaging of works by Graham, Limón and Taylor, as well as classics like Doris Humphrey's *The Shakers* (1931, restaged for LCDS by Ernestine Stodelle in 1985), has inclined in the 21st century towards commissioning contemporary choreographers like Tony Adigun, Julie Cunningham, Shobana Jeyasingh, and Ben Wright, and other artists who push the frontiers of dance. Not that the rich heritage of contemporary dance is ignored. Staging a Merce Cunningham *Event* for 3rd year students in April 2019 was the former Cunningham Company dancer and his Rehearsal Assistant, Jeannie Steele, a member of the LCDS Faculty and one of a small number of people licensed to remount the choreographer's work.[29]

Robin Howard, the founder of the School, The Place and CDT, would no doubt approve both of the traditions which the School has maintained and the need to move with the times. As he said as early as 1969, the goal was to give 'the maximum encouragement to young creative and performing artists. The aim was, and is, to develop a genuine British contemporary dance but not introverted. Whilst firmly rooted here it must remain international and continue to cooperate with the other arts and it must reflect the world outside.'[30]

That ambition was further underlined with his words from 1971, quoted earlier: 'I am hoping a large number of good dancers and choreographers will start up their own companies. We ought in this country to have small dance groups in at least six places in this country. Only once that happens and once some of them say that we are doing things in all the wrong ways – that we are too old-fashioned – only then, I think, will we have succeeded in what we are trying to do here.' With the increasing diversity and expansion of contemporary dance companies based in the UK, many of them gaining support from the Arts Council of England and other subsidising bodies in the UK, it is fair to say that his modest ambitions have been significantly exceeded.

Yet his enthusiasm for dance as an art form went far deeper than simply establishing its presence in the world. Siobhan Davies, reflecting on her first-hand experience of Howard, points to his belief that art should be an expression of humanity that enriches the world: 'his great concern was to make quite sure that the best of our human qualities are fully at work. He came out of a war, and, I think, he was seeing the world and wanted it to re-build itself up through creative, not negative means. In that sense

I've borrowed some of his fire. I believe in our whole intelligence, where the difference between mind and body is dissolved, and that dance is a site for this to be revealed. While theatre and education can play a big role in how dance works and is perceived, we (who work with and in dance) can also be present in many other situations and have useful dialogues with architects through to zoologists. We don't need to be framed by anything, but we are in and of the world and we can be a force.'[31]

The former Chief Executive Kenneth Olumuyiwa Tharp also remembered the depth of Howard's motivation: 'although it may look and feel very different I think the vision is still there in a number of ways. In the back of my notebook on the 20th September 1978, it says Robin Howard and then it says four words underneath: "quality, professionalism, love and service". Those were the things that Robin talked about as values and I think essentially those ingredients are still very much at the heart of the way we do things. I don't think Robin was ever afraid of change, in fact he was often the one to instigate it, and Bob too, but I think for me values are long lasting, they are not things you change easily.'[32]

There's no doubt that Howard's expression of 'love' sits less easily in the competitive entrepreneurial world, but that commitment to and passion for dance as well as Howard's principal values continue to underscore the work of LCDS. Sending the 2018 graduates on their way Clare Connor said: 'we stand on the shoulders of a great many artists here at London Contemporary Dance School. The graduates from the class of 2018 are no exception and amongst some of the most successful in their career destinations in recent years. In my first year as Chief Executive and Principal it has been an immense privilege to celebrate their skilful creativity and artistry. As our alumni we will look to them for their leadership and their challenge and along with the rest of the faculty I wish them the very best as they take the next steps into the future.'[33]

1   On 8 October 2018, The Place announced that the Richard Alston Dance Company would close in 2020. In April 2018, Alston stepped down from his role as Artistic Director of the Place. He was knighted for his services to Dance, Children and Young People in the 2019 New Year Honours.

2   Interview with Connor, 15 February 2018. HEFCE was replaced by the Office for Students in April 2018.

3   Ibid.

4   Ibid.

5   Ibid.

6   Interview with Connor, 15 February 2018

7   LCDS 'Graduating students', 2017

8   Siobhan Davies Dance (nd)

9   Interview with Davies, 30 January 2018

10   Ibid.

11   interview with Cousins, 4 October 2018

12   Ibid.

13   CAT stands for the Place's Centre for Advanced Training, which is part of a national intensive dance programme for 11-18 year olds who display exceptional potential and passion for dance.

14   Interview with Cousins, 4 October 2018

15   Interview with Connor, 15 February 2018

16   'London Contemporary Dance School at The Place' in LCDS Prospectus 2019/20

17   'London Contemporary Dance School BA (Hons) Contemporary Dance' in LCDS Prospectus 2019/20

18   Flying Low is an energetic and physically demanding contemporary dance training style developed by the Venezuelan dancer and choreographer David Zambrano. It is taught at LCDS by Leila McMillan, a specialist in the work who regularly gives workshops in the technique throughout the UK at places such as Trinity Laban, Rambert School of Ballet & Contemporary Dance, and Northern School of Contemporary Dance

19   LCDS graduating students 2018

20   Interview with Connor, 15 February 2018

21   Ibid.

22   Interview with Alex Graham, 5 December 2017. Alex Graham retired from LCDS in August 2019.

23 Conservatoire for Dance and Drama

24 Which? University – Dance Courses 2019

25 Interview with Alex Graham, 5 December 2017

26 The Place, July 2018

27 Ohno danced with Ohad Naharin's Batsheva Dance Company from 1998-2004. Gaga technique was developed by Naharin, and is a form of movement research designed to access an ever-expanding range of physicality through the imagery of sensation

28 Quoted in the New York Times review of documentary film 'Mr Gaga' by Glenn Kenny, 31 January 2017.

29 Jeannie Steele was a member of the Merce Cunningham Dance Company from 1993-2005, and his rehearsal assistant from 2001-2006. She continues to stage Cunningham's work internationally, and is Head of Technique and Performance at LCDS.

30 Howard in Adshead and Mansfield 1985, p.4

31 Interview with Davies, 30 January 2018

32 Interview with Tharp, 8 July 2015

33 The Place 2018

Bibliography

Adshead, J. and Mansfield, R. (1985). *London Contemporary Dance Theatre 1967-1975*. Surrey: NRCD.

Alexander, K. (2016). Interview at Siobhan Davies Studios, 28 July

Alston, R. (2000). 'Interview with Richard Alston.' Available from: www.thealstonstudio.com.

Alston, R. (2015). Interview, London Contemporary Dance School, 10 August

Anna Sokolow at The Place 1971 on Vimeo available from https://vimeo.com/9045983

Anon. (2006). 'Feature: Robert Cohan & Darshan Singh Bhuller.' Available from:http://londondance.com/articles/features/robert-cohan-and-darshan-singh-bhuller/

Brandstrup, K. (2015). *Private Passions*. BBC Radio 3, 1 November

Charrington, P. (2015). Interview, London, 29 January

Clarke, M. and C. Crisp (1989). *London Contemporary Dance Theatre*. London: Dance Books.

Cohan, R. (2015). Interview, London, 18 August

Conservatoire for Dance and Drama (2019). 'About us.' Available from: www.cdd.ac.uk/about-us/

Connell, P. (2015). Interview, London Contemporary Dance School, 20 September

Connor, C. (2018). Interview, London Contemporary Dance School, 15 February

Contemporary Dance Trust Archives – Archives Hub available at V&A Theatre Museum

Coton, A.V. (1954). 'Martha Graham in London.' *Dancing Times*. New series, 523, pp.407-408; 414.

Davies, S. and Lee, R. (2011). 'Gill Clarke.' Available from: www.independentdance.co.uk/author/gill-clarke/

Davies, S. (2018). Interview, Siobhan Davies Dance, 30 January

Devlin, G. (1989). *Cultural trends*. Vol. 1 Pt. 3, pp.45-56. Available from: http://www.bl.uk/reshelp/atyourdesk/docsupply/help/terms/index.html

Dodge, L. (2015). 'Nurturing the individual.' *Dancing Times 105*, 1260, pp.31-33.

Donnelly, A. (2015). Interview, London Contemporary Dance School, 22 October

Dudley, J. (1999). LCDS oral recollections transcribed by Sallie Bhuller (authors' collection)

Duke, B. (2018). Interview, London Contemporary Dance School, 1 March

Drummond, J. (1996). 'A golden stage.' *Dance Theatre Journal 13*, 12, pp.10-12.
Eager, J. (2015). Interview, Somerset, 20 July
Flatt, K. (2016). Interview, London Contemporary Dance School, 12 February
Frankenhaeuser, A. (2016). Email communication, 25 June
Graham, A. (2017). Interview, London Contemporary Dance School, 5 December
Hamilton, J. (2011). 'Chapter 4: 'Can't...try...can.' In Lansley, J. and F. Early, (eds).*The wise body*. Bristol: Intellect, pp.61-71.
Hamilton, J. (undated). 'Bio' julyenhamilton.com
Harding-Irmer, P. (2016). Email communication, 25 June
Hennessy, K. (undated) 'The experiment called contact improvisation'. Available from:http://www.foundsf.org/index.php?title=The_Experiment_Called_Contact_Improvisation
Hodes, S. (2002). 'Stuart Hodes.' In Horosko, M. (ed.). *Martha Graham: The evolution of her dance theory and training revised edition.* USA: University of Florida Press, pp.66-72.
Hoyle, S. (2017). 'My gurus.' Available from: www.artsprofessional.co.uk/magazine/my-gurus-sue-hoyle/sue-hoyle
Jackson, P. (2013). *The Last Guru.* London: Dance Books.
Jennings, L. (2015). 'The struggle for the soul of British dance.' Available from: www.theguardian.com
Johnston, P. (2015). *Nina Fonaroff – Life and art in dance.* Knoxville, Tennessee: Celtic Cat Publishing.
Jordan, S. (1992). *Striding out.* London: Dance Books.
Knight, J. (2015). Interview, London, 28 September
Lawrance, M. (2015). Interview, London Contemporary Dance School, 10 August
Lewis, V. (2015). Interview, London Contemporary Dance School, 16 October
Levene, L. (1994). 'And so they face the final curtain: London Contemporary Dance Theatre turn into the Richard Alston Dance Company.' *The Independent* Thursday 16 June. Available from: www.independent.co.uk
London Contemporary Dance School presents Collaborations 2016. Available from: https//www.theplace.org.uk/whats-on/collections/london-contemporary-dance-school-presents-collaborations-2016
London Contemporary Dance School virtual open day 2014. Available on Youtube
London Contemporary Dance School virtual open day 2015. Available on Youtube
London Contemporary Dance School (2017). 'Graduating students.'

Available from: https://www.lcds.ac.uk/sites/default/files/downloads/London%20Contemporary%20Dance%20School%20Graduating%20Students%202017.pdf

LCDS graduating students 2018. Available from: http://docplayer.net/100633249-London-contemporary-dance-school-graduating-students-lcds-ac-uk-lcdschool.html

London Contemporary Dance School (2018). 'Our vision.' Available from: https//www.lcds.ac.uk/our-vision

Mackrell, J. (1992). *Out of line.* London: Dance Books.

Mackrell, J. (2000). 'Duet for an odd couple.' Available from: https://www.theguardian.com/culture/2000/apr/11/artsfeatures2

Mackrell, J. (2010). 'The Place: dreams in a drill hall. Available from: https://www.theguardian.com/stage/2010/may/11/contemporary-dance-the-place

Mackrell, J. (2015). 'Are British dancers really outclassed on the world stage? *The Guardian.* Available from: www.theguardian.com

MacLennan, S. (2016). Interview, London, 21 April

Mansfield, R. (1985). 'London Contemporary Dance Theatre'. In White, J. (ed.). *20th Century Dance in Britain: A history of five dance companies.* London: Dance Books, pp.111-142.

McKim, R. (ed.). (2004). 'Introduction: Concerning what the London Contemporary Dance Theatre inherited.' In McKim, R. (ed.), *The essential inheritance of London Contemporary Dance Theatre.* Hampshire: Dance Books, pp.1-9.

McKim, R. (ed.). (2004). 'Dancing with Siobhan Davies/Awareness and Robin Howard: An interview with Sean Feldman.' In McKim, R. (ed.), *The essential inheritance of London Contemporary Dance Theatre.* Hampshire: Dance Books, pp.53-58.

McKim, R. (ed.). (2004). 'A dance family, a humane dance technique and what Robert Howard wanted: An interview with Janet Eager.' in McKim, R. (ed.), *The essential inheritance of London Contemporary Dance Theatre.* Hampshire: Dance Books, pp.91-98.

Meisner, N. (2013). 'Nina Fonaroff.' Available from http://www.indepdendent.co.uk/news/obituaries/nina-fonaroff-37032.html

Morris, G. and Nicholas, L. (2018). 'Introduction to Part 2'. In Morris, G. and L. Nicholas (eds). *Rethinking dance history.* London: Routledge, pp. 109-113.

Namron (2018). Interview, London Contemporary Dance School. 7 June

Neelands, J., G. Lindsay, V. Freakley, et al (2006). 'Drama and dance scheme. Evaluation project. Phase ll. Final report, March 2006'. Available from: www.warwick.ac.uk/fac/soc/cedar/projects/completed06/dadaeval2/finaldada.pdf

Nicholas, L. (2007). *Dancing in Utopia: Dartington Hall and its Dancers.* London: Dance Books.

Nodine, R. (2018). Interview, London Contemporary Dance School, 6 November

Parry, J. (1994). 'London Contemporary Dance Theatre.' *Dancing Times* 84, 1000, pp.338-339.

Parry, J. (2016). 'Kim Brandstrup – choreographer.' Available from: https://dancetabs.com/2016/02/kim-brandstrup-choreographer-2/

Powell, K. (2001). 'A sense of place.' *Architects Journal* – 18 October. Available from: https://www.architectsjournal.co.uk/home/a-sense-of-place/184828.article

Pritchard J. (2010). 'A history of The Place'. Available from: https://www.theplace.org.uk/history-place

Ralph, R. (1995). 'Change and development at The Place.' *Dancing Times* 1014, 75, pp.597;599.

Ralph, R. (1997). 'Peter Brinson.' *Dance Research.* 15, 1, pp.25-30.

Ralph, R. (2000). 'Degrees for professional dancers: Some personal reflections.' *Dancing Times 91*, 1081, pp.56-57.

Ralph, R. (2015). Interview, London Contemporary Dance School, 20 June

Robertson, A. (undated). 'Susan McGuire talks with Allen Robertson.' Available from http://www.danceconsortium.com/features/interview/talking-paul-taylor-with-allen-robertson/ February 8, 2016

Siobhan Davies Dance. 'Independent dance.' Available from: https://www.siobhandavies.com/independent-dance/1

Singh Bhuller, D. (2004). 'Robert Cohan eightieth birthday tribute,' *Dance Research, 22.* 2, pp.139-152.

Slayton, J. (2006). *The Prickly Rose – a biography of Viola Farber.* Bloomington, Indiana: Authorhouse.

Stainsby, H. (2015). Interview, London Contemporary Dance School, 1 July

Steele, D. (2016). Interview, London Contemporary Dance School, 6 September

Sunday Express (2005) 'Dance review: Collaborations by the London Contemporary Dance School. Availabe from: http://www.express.co.uk/entertainment/theatre/624272/Dance-review-Collaborations-London-Contemporary-Dance-School

Tamen, I. (2015). Interview, London Contemporary Dance School, 1 July

Tharp, Kenneth Olumuyiwa (2015). Interview, London Contemporary Dance School, 8 July

The Place (2018). 'Celebrating the success of London Contemporary Dance School's recent and continuing graduates'. Available from:

www.theplace.org.uk/blog/place-blog/celebrating-success-london-contemporary-dance-school%E2%80%99s-recent-graduates

Van Laast, A. (2016). Interview, London, 19 May

Which?University – Dance Courses (2019). 'Search for all courses'. Available from https://university.which.co.uk/subjects/dance?gclid=EAIaIQobChMI1-bFn7zM3QIVRjbTCh3EmgfTEAAYASAAEgLM4_D_BwE

Young, C. (2013). 'Reflections on Gerda Geddes.' *Body, Movement and Dance in Psychotherapy*. Available at: http://dx.doi.org/10.1080/17432979.2013.810665

Index

4D, 66, 73, 76
Adeline Genée Theatre, 20-21
Agis, Gaby, 87
Adigun, Tony, 99
Ailey, Alvin, 8, 16, 26, 32. Dance works: *Hermit Songs*, 26
Airs, (chor. Taylor), 71
Alexander, Kirsty, 83; becomes Assistant Director, 87
Alexander technique, 87
Allies and Morrison (architects), 79, 83
Alston, Sir Richard, 3, 80, 81, 87, 92; and Berners Place, 11-13; and Hutchinson, 14; and Artists' Rifles Drill Hall, 24-26; and New Cinema Club, 28-29; and teaching choreography, 36; and X-Group 39; and Strider, 44; and Travis Kemp/Molly Lake, 46; and Dartington, 63; appointed Artistic Director of CDT, 76-79; founding of Richard Alston Dance Company, 76, see also ftnt.1, p.100. Dance works: *Transit* 16, *Nowhere Slowly*, *Shiftwork* 36, *Dumka* 49, *Rainbow Bandit* 75, *Overdrive* 96
Anderson, Lea, 66
Appalachian Spring, (chor. Martha Graham), 7
Archer, Janet, 93
Architects' Journal, 81
Artists' Place Society, 27
Artists' Rifles Drill Hall, Dukes Rd (later known as The Place), 24-26
Arts Council of Great Britain, later Arts Council England; 35, 67, 79, 80, 93, 99 withholding grant, 25; funding increase, 27; ends funding for LCDT, 75; support for RADC, 76; Sue Hoyle former Director of Dance at ACE, 81; support for 'programme of change', 82
Arts Educational Trust, 9
Arts Fission Dance Company, 97
Ashford, John, 67, 76, 81
Ashory, Dorna, 96
Attenborough, Richard, 82

Balanchine, George, 38
Ballet for All, 15, 21
Ballet Rambert, 8, 46
Banner, Chris, 23,
Bannerman, Christopher, 58
Bannerman, Richard, 24
Barter, Nick, 82
Batsheva Company, 32, 98
Bausch, Pina, 62, 67
Beattie, Alan, 15
Berners Place, 2, 3-4, 20, 23, 25, 26, 32, 33, 36, 37, 43; description and early student experience, 11-16, see Alston, Davies, van Laast
Breakin' Convention, 92
Birtwistle, Harrison, 21, 28
Blacking, Professor John, 53
Bland, Alexander, 21
Boman, Primavera, 15
Bonachela, Rafaela, 96
Bonnie Bird Prize for Choreography; see Greenhough, 73
Bougaard, Corrinne, 32

Bourne, Matthew, 54; and *Swan Lake*, 95, see Cousins
Brandstrup, Kim, 3, 44, 51, 61, 72
Brinson, Peter 21, 53
Bristol Old Vic, 83
Burnie, David, 81, *see also* ftnt.12, p.84
Butcher, Rosemary, 87

Cabrelli's Café, 16, 23
California Institute of the Arts, 66
Candoco, 39, 92
Canterbury Cathedral performance, 58
Casey, Maria, 15
Cecchetti technique, 33
Cell, (chor. Cohan), 26, 27
Central School of Ballet, 47, 83
Challis, Chris, 39
Charrington, Pernille, 48-49; and Fonaroff and Lonnroth, 64
Chediny, Antonin, 89
Cheshire Dance Workshop, 80
Chiesa, Norberto, 18, 20, 25, 27, 35
Christopher, Patricia, 8
Circus Space, 83
Clarke, Gill, 86, 87, *see also* Davies and Lee
Clarke, Mary, 3
CNAA (Council for National Academic Awards) 39, 53,
Cohan, Sir Robert, 3, 48, 58, 65, 67, 83, 87, 94, 98, 100; first meetings with Howard, 6-7; arrival at LCDS, 18; teaching, 19, *see* Davies; prepares first performance, 20; first performance by Contemporary Dance Group, 21-22; description, 23, *see* van Laast; need for a permanent base, 23; moves to London, 24; 25; first season of LCDT, 26-7; teaching with Dudley, 33-34; encourages student choreography, 36; teaching choreography, 38, *see* Horst; financial crisis, 43, *see* Harrison; Residencies, 45; degree, 55, *see* Ralph; degree, 57, *see* Frankenhaeuser; Cohan-Graham technique, 61; inner transformation, 64, *see* McKim; retires as Artistic Director of LCDT 68; *see also* ftnt.42, p.70. Dance works: *Hunter of Angels, Tsaikerk, Eclipse, Sky*, 25, *Cell*, 27; *Stages*, 35, see van Laast), *Khamsin* 45, *Stabat Mater* 58, 65
Collins, Aletta, 3, 74, 92
Connell, Peter, 46, 48, 61, 79; and degree, 54; and loosening of Graham influence 63, 72; and closure of LCDT, 75
Connor, Clare, 100; appointed Chief Executive CDT, 92; personal background, 93; Interim Principal, 93; her first prospectus on the breadth of the organisation and enriching the programme 96-97
Conservatoire of Dance and Drama (CDD), 82, 83, 93, 97, 98; *see also* Lewis
Contact Improvisation, 4, 63, 72, 87, 96, 98; analysis, 88, *see* Nodine
Contemporary Ballet Trust (forerunner of Contemporary Dance Trust), 2, 20
Contemporary Dance Group, 20-21
Contemporary Dance Trust (CDT), 29, 34, 43, 66, 75, 76, 81,

82, 96, 99; and role of 2-3; securing freehold of The Place and Flaxman Terrace, 49; removing Howard as Chairman, 67; Connor appointed Chief Executive, 92
Contraction, 19-20, *see* Graham technique
Coventry Centre for Performing Arts, 52
Cousins, James, 95
Creative Industries Federation (CIF), 97
Crisp, Clement, 3
Cunningham, Julie, 99
Cunningham, Merce, 1, 7, 8, 16, 35, 36, 62, 74, 96, 98, 99
Cushman, Flora, 39

Dance and Dancers, 12
Dance and Drama Awards, 82
Dance One, Two, Four, 20
Dance Umbrella, 48
Dancing To Music, (chor. Marks), 72
Dandeker-Arnold, Celeste, 23, 39, 92; *see also* Candoco
Darrell, Peter, 8
Dartington College of Arts, 63
Davies Siobhan (Sue), 3, 21, 24, 53, 64, 80, 92, first class and impression of Robin Howard, 15; and impact of Cohan, 19; and obituary of Gill Clarke, 86-87; and changes in dancers' opportunities, 94-95; Howard's vision and the place of dance, 99-100; *see also* Siobhan Davies Dance, Siobhan Davies Company, Siobhan Davies Studios
Diversion of Angels, (chor. Martha Graham), 7
Drogheda, Lord, 44

Dudley, Jane, 35, 40, 45, 46, 48, 54, 61, 62, 64, 65, 68, 93, and early career, 32; appointment as Director of Dance Studies, 33; and Cohan, 33; and teaching principles, 34; and Fonaroff 37, 39; and degree, 55; retires as Director of Dance Studies, 71. Dance works: *Harmonica Breakdown* 32
Dumka, (chor. Alston), 49
Duncan, Clare, 13, 22, 39, 45, 53
Duke, Ben, 3, 87; and Nodine, 88; and Lost Dog Company, 89
Dunn, Margaret, 56, 61, 80
Dunkley, Chris, 56
DV8, 67,76

Eager, Janet, ('Mop'); becomes Howard's assistant, 6; and earliest classes, 8-9; and Berners Place, 11-12; and finding The Place, 24, 26; and the press conference at The Place, 25; and financial problems, 27; and need for degree, 52, 58; and the removal of Howard as Chairman, 68
Early, Fergus, 36
Eclipse, (chor. Cohan), 20
EdGE and EDGE, 66, 97
Edinburgh Festival, 48
Elizabethan Rooms, 5
El Penitente, (chor. Martha Graham), 26, 27, 38
Emblen, Ronald, 74
Errand Into The Maze, (chor. Martha Graham), 7
Explorations, 26
English Dance Theatre, 48
Esplanade, (chor. Paul Taylor), 71
Evelyn, Mary, 65, 93

Extemporary Dance Theatre, 81, *Family of Man*, (chor. Mittelholzer), 20

Farber, Viola; and loosening influence of Graham, 62-63
Feldenkrais technique, 87
Feldman, Sean; and Dudley 33, 62; and Robin's Course, 64
Financial Times, 67
Finnissy, Michael, 15, 37
Fisher, Juliet, 45, 62, 73, 74, 93, see ftnt. 8, p.69
Fitzgerald, Robert, 27
Flatt, Kate, 48, 92; and Dudley, 33; and Fonaroff, 38; background and engagement with Graham technique, 44-45; and CNAA, 53, 92
Flaxman Terrace, 1, 3, 49; CDT acquires freehold, 43; and first rebuilding 46; second rebuilding and new entrance, 81
Flying Low technique, 1, 96, *see also* ftnt.18, p.101
Fokine, Vera, 38
Fonaroff, Nina, 32, 40, 48, 54, 64, 68 appointed Head of Choreography, 37; and attitude to teaching, 38 (*see also* Horst); and Dudley, 39; retires from LCDS, 72
Frankenhaeuser, Anca, 27, 92, 93; and Howard 23; and the X-Group 39; and degree, 57; and graduation, 58
Frayling, Christopher, 56
Freakley, Vivienne, 74
Fulkerson, Mary; and Release, 63, 72

Gable, Christopher, 47

Gaga technique, 98-99
Geddes, Gerda, 'Pytt', 98; and Tai Chi 63-64 (*see also* Charrington and Tharp)
Gibbs, Linda, 45, 48, 75
Gibson, Lord, 43
Gielgud, Sir John, 3
Gilgren, Hannah, 74
Givens, Craig, 44
Goodman, Lord, 26
Gore Hotel, 5
Graham, Alex, 97, 98
Graham, Martha, 1, 3, 12, 16, 22, 26, 33, 35, 45, 48, 62, 63, 65, 66, 87, 98; and the first London season, 6-7; and student scholarships, 8-9; and releasing Cohan,18; and technique, 19-20; ends patronage, 61; *see also* Graham technique, Martha Graham Dance Company. Dance works: *Appalachian Spring, Diversion of Angels, Errand Into The Maze*, 7, *Letter to the World*, 3, *El Penitente*, 26, 38, *Primitive Mysteries*, 38
Graham technique; first demonstration of Graham technique in London, 8; demonstration of Graham class, 13; Cohan's approach to first students, 19; the contraction, 19-20; Cohan's approach with Dudley, 33-34; Flatt's experience of Graham, 45; Cohan's own style of Graham, 61; on Dudley's approach to Graham, 62; and Fisher's, 62, 73, 74; and Farber's opposition to Graham and loosening influence, 62-63; 'inner transformation', 64-65
Gravetye Manor, 5

Greenhough, Karen, 72-73
Gulbenkian Foundation, 25, 27, 40

Hall, Fernau, 15
Hamilton, Julyen; and Strider, 44
Hanna, Thomas, 63
Harding-Irmer, Patrick; 92; and the X-Group, 39-40; and degree, 57-58
Harewood, Earl of, 3
Harmonica Breakdown, (chor. Dudley), 32
Harper, Peggy, 6
Harrison, Gabriel, 43, 44
HEFCE (Higher Education Funding Council England), 3, 93, 97; and CDD, 82
Henry, Jenny, 56, 57
Herdman, Alan; and Pilates, 27, 48
Hermit Songs, (chor. Ailey), 26
Hinkson, Mary, 8
Stuart Hodes; and Contraction, 20
Holger, Hilda, 15
Holm, Hanya, 24
Horst, Louis; choreographic teaching system, 37, 39
Horta, Rui, 76
Horton, Lester, 7
Howard, Robin, 2, 3, 72, 75; and personal life 5; and first encounter with Martha Graham Company and Cohan, 6-7; encouragement from Marie Rambert, 7; student scholarships to Martha Graham School, 8; Graham's prediction, 9; Berners Place, 11-13; appoints Hutchinson, 14; invitation to Cohan, 18; first performances at Adeline Genée Theatre, 20, 21; impression by Frankenhaeuser, 23; finds and negotiates lease for Dukes Rd premises, 24; press conference to announce plans, 25; sale of vintage cars, 27; financial problems, 25, 27, 44, 66; commitment to the avant-garde, 26, 29, 35; ambitions, 34, 40, 49; sale of personal collections, 44; acquires freehold of The Place and Flaxman terrace premises, 44; need for proper qualification and phone call to Ralph, 52; CNAA, 53; degree, 58; School's own teachers, 61; Robin's Course, 64; letter to Financial Times, 67; removed as Chairman by CDT board, 67; death, 68; on dance and the dancer, 90; Connor's reminiscence, 93; 99, *see* Davies; 100, *see* Tharp; *see also* Robin Howard Dance Theatre, Robin Howard Trust
Hoyle, Sue, 8, 83; appointed General Manager, later Executive Director, 81; takes charge of rebuilding and expansion, 81
Hribar, Xenia, 13, 22
Hukam, Gurnit, 49
Humphrey, Doris, 7; and restaging of *The Shakers,* 99
Hunter of Angels, (chor. Cohan), 20
Hutchinson-Mackenzie, Pat, 15, 16, 23, 44, 46; appointed Principal, 14; teaching and auditions, 14, *see* Alston and van Laast, 14; demonstrating ballet technique 37, *see* Alston; retires as Principal 40

ILEA (Inner London Education

Authority), 40, 80
Independent Dance, 94
Institute of Choreology, 80
Institute of Psychosynthesis, 46
International Theatre Institute (ITI), 68
Isaacson, Laurence, 75

Jarman, Derek, 26
Jennings, Luke, 83
Jeyasingh, Shobana, 99
Johnson Small, Jamila, 90
Johnston, Phillip, 38
Jonzi D, 92
Jordan, Stephanie, 25, 36
Judson Dance Theater Movement, 36, 72
Juilliard School, 66
Junction, (chor. Taylor), 71
Just Us Dance Theatre, 90

Kay, Rosie, 3
Kelly, Brigitte, 14
Khan, Akram, 89
Kehlior, Peter, 48
Kemp, Travis, 46
Kent, University of, 54, 55
Kerrigan, Conor, 96
Khamsin, (chor. Cohan), 45
Kings Cross Partnership, 81
Kirkpatrick, Charlotte, 57, 58
Knight, Judyth; and the Graham School, 13; and Dudley, 34; and closure of LCDT, 75, *see* ftnt.11, p.17
Kundalini yoga, 64

Laast, van Anthony (see under Van Laast)
Laban (Trinity Laban), 65, 73, 80, 87, 89
Lake, Molly, 46, 48

LAMDA, 23, 83
Lamford, Tim, 64
Lansley, Jacky, 37, 40, 92
Lansley, Paula, 39
Lapsezon, Noemi, 45, 48, and performing at Adeline Genée Theatre 20-21
Lawrance, Martin; and McGuire 71; and school curriculum and streaming, 73-74; and degree, 74-75; and closure of LCDT, 75; and RADC, 76
Lee, Jayne, 48
Lee, Rosemary, 86
Lehtinen, Ritva, 29
Letter to the World, (chor. Martha Graham), 32
Leverhulme Trust, 66
Lewis, Veronica; appointed Principal, 80; and the rebuilding, 81; and the creation of the CDD, 82-83; developing shared responsibility between students and the faculty, 86; moving forward 87, *see* Alexander; retires as Principal, 93
Liburd, Paul, 74
Limited Dance Company, 40
Limón, José 7, 65, 74
Logan, Peter, 26
London Contemporary Dance Group, 21, 29
London Contemporary Dance School (LCDS), formerly known as The London School of Contemporary Dance,

Choreographers trained at LCDS: *see* Alston, Brandstrup, Collins, Cousins, Davies, Duke, Flatt, Hamilton, Johnson-Small, Jonzi D, Kay, Lansley J, Lawrance, Moreland, Newson, Pita,

Recacha, Requhardt, Sikorski, Singh Bhuller, Toonga, Van Laast, Wellesley Wesley, Wilton

Conservatoire for Dance and Drama: see Attenborough, Barter, LAMDA, Lewis, Myerscough, Ralph

Dance and Choreography Teachers: see Alston, Cohan, Connell, Cousins, Dudley, Duncan, Early, Emblen, Evelyn, Farber, Fisher, Flatt, Fonaroff, Geddes, Gibbs, Greenhough, Hinkson, Horst, Hutchinson, van Laast, Lapsezon, Lake, Lansley J., Lapsezon, Lonnroth, Louther, MacLennan, Mattox, McGuire, McKim, Mittelholzer, Nodine, North, Ohno, Posner, Powell, Quirey, Ross, Scott, Stainsby, Steele J., Williams, Winter, Yuriko

Funding and Finance: see Arts Council; see Howard 25, 27, 44, 67; see Cohan, 43; see Gulbenkian Foundation; see Kings Cross Partnership, see Lottery

Honours Degree: acquisition of 52-58, see also CNAA, Kent; 66; and Lawrance's experience 74-75; and Connor 93; and Taught Degree Awarding Powers 97-98

Premises: Berners Place 2, 3-4, 11-15, 23, 32, 33, 43; The Place (Artists' Rifles/Dukes Rd) 1-2, 24-29, 32, 43-49, 76, 79-83, 93, 99; Flaxman Terrace 1, 3, 43, 46, 49, 81

Principals: see Hutchinson-Mackenzie, Howard, Kemp, Ralph, Marchant, Lewis, Connor

Student funding: international expansion 66; and Leverhulme Trust, 66; towards the CDD, 81-82, see also Lewis, HEFCE, CDD; and Office for Students, 97

London Contemporary Dance Theatre (LCDT) also described as the Company, 12, 13, 14, 21, 32, 33, 35, 36, 39, 53, 58, 66, 67, 73, 74, 76, 80, 92, 94; first performances at The Place, 26; and Residencies, 45; inspiration to students, 65; Cohan retires as Artistic Director, 68; closure, 75

London Festival Ballet, 81

Lonnroth, Ingegerd, 48, 49

Lost Dog Company, 89

Lottery, National; funding for redevelopment, 79

Louther, William, 12, 23, 64

Lunn, Jonathan, 49, 62

Lyons, Jacqui, 13

MacLennan, Sue, 79, 88, 89, see also ftnt.5, p.84

Maler, Leopold, 26

Marchant, Graham, 76, 77, 79, 80

Markova-Dolin Company 46

Marks, Victoria, 72

Marowitz, Charles, 29

Martha Graham Company, 3, 12, 21, 22, 23, 27, 32, 33, 37, 53 and 1954 London season & Howard's first encounter, 6-7; and teachers from, 8; and invitation to Cohan, 18

Matthew Bourne's New Adventures, 54, 76

Mattox, Matt, 32

Maxwell Davies, Peter, 28
McGregor, Wayne, 76, 80, 86, 95
McGuire, Susan, 73; joins as Head of Contemporary Dance Studies, 71; introduces Paul Taylor repertory, 71; five-year plan, 72; leaves, 79, 80
McKim, Ross, 45, 64, 65
Missa Brevis, (chor. José Limón), 65
Mercury Theatre, 9
Meseguer, Raquel, 89
Mittelholzer, Anna, 13, 18-19, 20, 21
Moore, Geoff, 29
Moore, Henry, 3
Moreland, Barry, 27
Morrice, Norman, 8
Mortimer, Isabel, 74
Mortimer, Michael, 25, 27
Moseley, Francesca, 95
Moving Being, 29
Mumford, Peter, 56
Museum of Modern Art, Oxford, 39
Musical Offering, (chor. Taylor), 71
Myerscough, John, 82

Naharin, Ohad, 96, 98
Namron 12, 13, 22, 29
Nelson, Jeremy, 49
New Cinema Club, 28-29
Newson, Lloyd, 66, 67, 89
Nexus, 93
Nodine, Rick; and Contact Improvisation, 88
Nora, 90
Nordi, Cleo, 28
North, Robert, 45, 48, 58
Northern School of Contemporary Dance, 73, 83, 89
Norton, Jack, 47, 66
Nowhere Slowly, (chor. Alston), 36

Office for Students, 97
Ohno, Chisato, 96, 98
Old Vic, 24
Oliver, Odette, 16
Olivier Award, 89
Overdrive, (chor. Alston), 96
Oyez House, 43

Parsons, Wayne, 96
PassoMezzo, (chor. Naharin), 96
Pavlova, Anna, 28, 46
Paxton, Steve, 63, 72, 88
Peggy Hawkins Gala Event, 96
Pellegrinni, Elisabetta, 96
Phoenix Dance Theatre, 33, 93
Piece for Metronome and Three Dancers, (chor. Steede), 15
Piece Period, (chor. Taylor), 12
Pierrot Players, 28
Pilates, 27, 28
Pita, Arthur, 65
Pite, Crystal, 97
The Place Prize 76, 89
Polaris, (chor. Pite), 97
Porter, Andrew, 53
Posner, Ruth, 12, 23
Potter, Lauren, 49, 62
Potter, Sally, 40
Powell, Kenneth, 81
Powell, Robert, 12, 20, 27, 33
Primitive Mysteries, (chor. Martha Graham), 38

Quirey, Belinda, 48, 53, 57

RADA (Royal Academy of Dramatic Art), 76, 82
Rainbow Bandit, (chor. Alston), 75
Ralph, Richard, 37, 47-48, 49, 68, 75, 82; engaged as Principal 52-53; and acquisition of degree, 53-56, *see* CNAA and

Kent University; international expansion, 66; contacts McGuire, 71; suggests grouping of schools, 76-77; resigns, 77
Rambert, Dame Marie; 3, 11, 47; influence on Howard, 7; heads committee 8
Rambert (Company), 75, 76, 89
Rambert School, 12, 14, 46-47, 83
Random Dance Company, 76
Recacha, Eva, 73
Release, 63, 72, 96
Requhardt, Frauke, 3, 73
Residencies, 32, 33, 80
Resolution, 2, 67, 73, 95
Reynolds, David, 18
Richard Alston Dance Company, 71, 76, 87
Riche, John, 37
Robin Howard Dance Theatre, 2, 3, 4, 83, 96
Robin Howard Trust, 8
Roope, Clover, 23, 26, see ftnt.5, p.30
Ross, Bertram, 8
Royal Academy of Dancing, 65
Royal Ballet, 53
Royal Ballet School, 33

Sadler's Wells, 75, 95, 97
Saint Martin's Art School, 15
Sarah, Peter, 76
Scott, Edith, 36
Schechter, Hofesh, 89
Shakers, The (chor. Humphrey), 99
Shiftwork, (chor. Alston), 36
Siobhan Davies Dance, 15
Siobhan Davies Company, 80, 86
Siobhan Davies Studios, 92
Sikorski, Eleanor, 90
Simpson, Kirstie, 88
Singh Bhuller, Dharshan, 45, 46, 49
Skillen, Suzanne, 16
Small, Michael, 58
Sky, (chor. Cohan), 20
Sokolow, Anna, 35
Somatics, 4, 45, 87
South Bank Centre, 93
Southwark Cathedral, 65
Spring Loaded, 2, 76
Staatsoper Bremerhaven, 98
Stabat Mater, (chor. Cohan), 58, 65
Stages, (chor. Cohan), 35
Stainsby, Hilary, 73, 79, 86
Stannard, Ann, 47
Stark-Smith, Nancy, 88
State University of Purchase, New York, 66
Steede, Patrick, 20
Steele, David, 83, 89
Steele, Jeannie, 99
Stodelle, Ernestine, 99
Stratford Circus Arts Centre, 93
Strider, 36, 44, 53, 63, 92
Stuart, Muriel, 38
Szekesfehervase Dance Company, 98

Tai Chi, 63, 98
Tamen, Isabel, 48, 65, 74, 98
Tanztheater Wuppertal, 48
Taught Degree Awarding Powers (TDAP), 97, 98
Taylor, Paul, 8, 13, 35, 66, 71. Dance works: *Airs, Esplanade, Musical Offering, Junction 71, see also* McGuire
Telesio, Franca, 23
Tharp, Kenneth Olumuyiwa, 66, 98; and student life in the late 1970s, 47-48; 49; and taking degree, 58; and Tai Chi, 64; and inspiration from LCDT, 65; leaves

position of Chief Executive, 92; and Howard's lasting vision, 100

Tharp, Twyla, 66

The Annunciation, (chor. North), 58

Theater St Gallen, 98

The Place, 1, 2, 3, 74, 75, 80, 93, 99; the move to The Place, 24; conversion of and naming The Place, 25-26; and official opening, 26; introduction of Pilates, 28, 29, 32; and threat to lease and purchase of freehold, 43-44; rebuilding in late 1970s, 46; host to Rambert School and Central School 47; John Ashford appointed Theatre Director, 76; Alston becomes Artistic Director and RADC is the new permanent company, 79; modernising, 81-83

The Sparse Collective, 89

Theatre and Artist Development, 83

The Times, 15

Titsa, Khin, 64

Tomlinson, Iris, 54

Toonga, Joseph, 89

Touch Wood, 2

Transit, (chor. Alston), 16

Transitions, 73

Trier, Carola, 27

Turkish National Ballet Company, 33

Tsaikerk, (chor. Cohan), 20

UK Provident Association, 43

Union Dance Company, 32

Valois, Dame Ninette de, 3, 11

Vallenkamp, Vasco, 48

Vandekeybus, Wim, 76

Van Laast, Anthony, 3, 27, 32, 35-36, 48, 92; and audition, 14; and the early curriculum, 15; and impact of Cohan, 23; and preparing The Place, 25; and learning to teach, 52

Verve, 73, 94

Victor Sylvester Ballroom, 9

Vic-Wells Ballet, 46

Wagoner, Dan, 35, 52, 74

Wain, John, 56

Waltz, Sasha, 76

Warwick Arts Centre, 52

Wellesley Wesley, Flora, 90

Western Theatre Ballet, 8

Westminster College, Oxford, 54

Which? University Guide, 98

White Heat, (chor. Wagoner), 74

Williams, Dudley, 23, 32

Wilton, James, 95

Winter, Ethel, 8, 12

Worth, Irene, 24

Wright, Ben, 99

Xinxin Song, 98

X6, 92

'X' Group, 39, 40, 97

Young Artists Platform of Dance, Beijing, 98

Yuriko, 12

Zappola Company, 98